RAMBLINGS OF A RESTLESS SOUL

Kenna Bifane

12/18/13

Ramblings of a Restless Soul

Kenna Lach Bifani

To order additional copies of this book, contact:
Xlibris Corporation
1-888-795-4274
www.Xlibris.com
Orders@Xlibris.com
104363

Special thanks to Betty Dunets for the support and feedback as I wrote, and to Kristina Bifani for the cover artwork.

Contents

INTRODUCTION

For as early as I can remember, I've dreamed of traveling and seeing the world. It may have been that my father told me of his adventures in the twenties and thirties, of getting on his bicycle and traveling hundreds and hundreds of miles. He later traded in the bicycle in for a small airplane; I remember the first as a Piper Cub. By the time I was ten, I had seen a lot of the Midwest of the States from the windows of a small airplane. There was also the memory of feeling like a prisoner at age two when I was diagnosed with tuberculosis, and the treatment at that time for young children was total bed rest for six weeks. My earliest memory is looking out that window of our house, watching everyone else running around the yard. My first remembered thought was "I'll never be caged up again."

As an adolescent, I was considered the "wild child" though the only girl in a family of five children. I went as far afield as I was allowed. In high school, it was a competitive band that traveled around the immediate states for competition and still in my dad's plane when I had the time and he had the space. I chose nursing as my major in college because it was a profession for women in which jobs were available everywhere around the globe. At nineteen, I moved to San Francisco—what seemed the other side of the planet to my parents—for university. Though I was a penniless student, I was always trying to plan a trip somewhere—Mexico, Hawaii. That was in the sixties, and when I graduated from university, all in my nursing class at graduation discussed our hopes and dreams. The others aspired for marriage, babies, and further education. I already had my foot out the door, looking for the next place to which I hadn't been. I applied for the Peace Corps, but they were far too slow with their application process. I was long gone by the time an offer was sent to me. It was for Iran and one of my few regrets. It's not the safest place to visit in today's world.

Several classmates had graduation gifts of two-week paid tours of Europe, and I thought "boring" and relatively predictable, and I never liked anything too predictable. I went immediately to work for a year and then bought a Eurail pass, the book *Europe on Five Dollars a Day*, and left for three months in Europe with no planned itinerary. I stayed at B&Bs and hostels and went wherever the wind took me. Other American women traveling alone on a totally unplanned itinerary were few and far between. As I didn't speak a foreign language at that time, I hooked up with mainly Canadians, Australians, New Zealanders, and Brits. There were times I was alone and others where I joined someone going to a place that sounded interesting. The train changed to hitchhiking, which was far more adventuresome; it was the people I met and the experiences of learning of the families and the culture and their interests. It was the fun of learning to communicate without the benefit of a common language and, more than anything, visiting places that were not on the standard tourist itinerary. I arrived at borders of what were then the "iron curtain" countries and, with a bit of finagling, entered a new and very different world.

I returned after the three months to San Francisco and immediately started making plans to hitchhike around the world with stops to live and work in Europe, South Africa, and Australia for a couple of years each. My parents' only hope was that I should meet a good man and settle. That was after all what I was being prepared for by attending university. To this day, I don't think they understand that incredible appetite I had and still have for travel and adventure, but the family has traveled vicariously through my adventures. They enjoy doing research and watch travel films relating to where I am going.

I spend a lot of time pondering over the reasons myself because forty years on, my feet are still itchy and the moss never grows under my feet. Is it genetics or the early experiences? I have the fantasy that our family genes trace back to Genghis Khan and Mongolia because the background is Slavic and there was that migration so many centuries ago. But my brothers have never had that same need, although several of their offspring have. On the other hand, I know many who were imprisoned in their childhood due to a debilitating illness and also do not have the same restlessness and curiosity as myself. I return home on visits and share my experiences. People ask questions, and their interest is piqued within five minutes.

There are many who do enjoy traveling, as long as it is "within the box." They go on a cruise annually and stop in several cities and several countries in between. I tried it once and felt as though I was one of a herd of cattle on a ship the size of a small city. In addition, the food was atrociously salty; and there was pushing to sell drinks, perfume, and art for high prices. I really felt like a prisoner. I don't belittle anyone for that style of seeing the world; it is indeed more secure and predictable. It was just never my style.

I think the bus tours or even the individually planned short-term adventures allow for a bit more, but not much more than the time needed to learn more than what the Eiffel Tower or London Eye see or feel like. Some of the tourists do not even have time to venture far enough to spend time with the people of the country other than their tour guides. And instead of trying the local foods, they look for McDonald's instead. It seems to me that most of the enjoyment in travel is learning about the culture and experiencing people different than myself.

There are those also who do live for longer periods of time in another country due to work, and their experience may be quite unique or they may experience it solely as an American. Some socialize only with the other Americans but do get out and experience different foods and surrounding countries and at least work with some from the culture in which they are living. I've met few who do not gain from and love the experience. Shopping for groceries and getting things in a home repaired become experiences when abroad.

I have traveled in all of these modes, and the most meaningful for me have been the travels of the past fifteen years when I stepped all the way out of the box. I started backpacking again then after a divorce and had some supporters as well as those friends who thought I had lost my marbles. I have never looked back as these adventures have made me feel as I grow older that I still don't know everything; there is still so much to learn and it helps me keep young at heart. In the beginning, I kept diaries; but once I became a bit more adept with computers, I started writing newsletters and attaching them. Many friends have said to me, "You must write a book" and "Don't cross me off your list please." I thank them for their persistence. I have spent many a day or night sitting with a group of people, each from a different part of the globe deep in the same kind of discussions that I might have back in the U.S. I have learned from them and treasure each and every one of them.

It's been a long time coming, and the travels themselves keep me from the concentration and the processing that need to happen. The stories are mainly from the past fifteen years, and the purpose is simply to share those experiences of people, countries, and events that were meaningful and different because they were from a vantage point outside of the box. There is no mention of real people or organizations by name because that is not the essence of the experience; the essence is the experience itself, whether it is a person or event or thought process in a different culture. In some instances, the person or event is totally fictional.

My final statement is to say that intraculturally, we are often more similar than different, especially when it relates to basic needs and feelings. We all develop along Maslow's "hierarchy of needs." There are horrid people in every country, and there are wonderful people in every country. I am thankful for all the wonderful people and sometimes even the horrid ones I have met along the way. They have given and are still giving me that insight.

The Secret Kingdom

Once upon a time and long ago, there were migrations of peoples all over the world. There was a nomadic tribe which traveled many miles over an extended period of time and came to the Western side of Java in Indonesia. The area was mountainous, covered in lush rain forest. The tribe found everything they needed for growing rice, their staple. The climate was ideal; there were the seasonal monsoon rains, and there were no aggressive people already settled there. And so they put up their tents and called it home. Their language was different from the other peoples in that land. They remained isolated into modern times, although the tents became huts and houses. Villages were developed with small shop centers. The rice fields were cultivated on the mountainsides, and a few people were delegated to leave the kingdom and travel to the outside villages and sell the rice for other staples. Otherwise, they were self-sustaining.

A king ruled peacefully. There were no wars; there was no contact with the world outside other than the rice peddlers. Everyone worked in harmony and cared for each other. There were no cars or buses; the mode of travel was trekking from village to village. The kingdom after all was perhaps not more than sixty kilometers in diameter. The life was extremely simple and, to outward appearances, idyllic. The king lived simply as well in a palace, which was a large wooden structure twice the size of a normal house with a smaller separate structure for his wife. It was not decorated with gold, and there were no guards with guns and uniforms surrounding the palace. It did have a forecourt where people would gather. The king and queen dressed in ordinary clothes; they were not fashion trendsetters. There was no pretense or show of power through wealth.

Each village had a village chief who was also the medicine man. A very basic medical system was put in place. It was a prevention model with the weekly screening of babies and young children with weights taken. When there was illness, traditional medicine and herbs were used. The population was generally healthy without malnutrition seen in poorer places. Death usually came with very old age or earlier from trauma—an old elephant on the rampage or a wild boar attack or a cobra bite. Anyone new to the village went first to the house of the village chief to introduce himself or to request permission to live in the village.

This is exactly how we found the kingdom when we arrived in the midnineties on a volunteer mission with a group of eighteen young students from England, doing community service in their gap year before commencing university. The group also included a doctor and nurse to deal with any maladies which might occur. The leader of the group had brought a very few other groups before after waiting hours initially to meet with the king and offer services. What a surprise to meet the king and sign in the registrar. Only thirty-five outsiders had visited the kingdom prior to us. The groups who came before had built schools for the villages. Our contract was to build a lookout shelter for the forest ranger that had the whole of the kingdom to watch over and the prevention of illegal logging and, of course, fires. We also needed to build a water reservoir for one village and do some general mapping.

The nomadic tribes have now existed for over four hundred eighty years, and though many speak Indonesian, most still use their original language. The population is approximately twenty-eight thousand, and there are twenty-eight villages in the kingdom. The people of the kingdom were extremely welcoming. Many had not had contact with white fellows on previous occasions, so they often followed us everywhere, including behind a tree to pee to see if we had the same body functions. This included not only the children but the adults as well. And it was not only the elimination; it was the bathing, the eating, the working, and the playing. Privacy is something we sacrificed for the experience. We normally set up camp in the rain forest and slept outside in hammocks with mosquito nets covering us. We dug our own latrines and then filled them in when we left so the area was unchanged. We bathed each day in the river and never looked in a mirror. We washed our clothes in the river as well, and in the beginning, some left their clothes hanging in a tree to dry only to find a monkey swinging from tree to tree in it the next morning. We trekked from village to village, sometimes up to twenty-five kilometers in a day. By the end of the day, we were exhausted in the tropical humid heat.

When we stayed in a village, the people of the village would open their houses to us. We went to the fields with the women and then later helped them pound the rice, with them smiling on. They taught us with great patience how to make baskets, which we needed to have when we built the reservoir to carry sand and rocks up from the river, again smiling. I'm sure it was because we made it look so difficult. One day, to our delight, we looked up to see a group of thirty young schoolchildren, all in their uniforms marching in line to help us. In the evening, when the work was done, we sat and watched them prepare the food around an open fire in the kitchen, the smoke exiting through a hole in the roof. We ate with them. The communication was more by gesturing and facial expressions because only our leader spoke their language and none of them spoke English. There was no electricity or plumbing, needless to say. But more than in other developing countries, there was a communal bathroom, which was a small high tub filled with water and a jug for pouring the water over oneself. The daily bathing was a ritual for the locals. Each afternoon as they were going to the river or wherever to bath, they would look at us and say, "Mandi?" the word for bath. The villages did have some very limited generator power for a few hours in the evening. Whether in the jungle or in the village, we ended the day writing in our diaries and reading and then falling asleep, exhausted.

There were unforgettable people and moments. There was the kind and gentle woman whose home we stayed in. She was twenty-nine and beautiful. She was a grandmother of a five-year-old. I'm sure we all had that look of shock on our faces. We were told that it was normal for girls to marry at fourteen or fifteen. All I could think was I was still wearing diapers at that age. I've since come to learn that that's probably the norm in at least fifty percent of the world. There were our local guides who would suddenly show up at the end of the day with treats off the trees, local foods and things like that, and I'm sure it wasn't in their job description. And there was the day I was called to come with a carrier cot to the river. Someone was face-down in the river. It was one of our local guides. We got him out; and luckily, he was conscious and breathing but also in shock. He had fallen in after a few too many Bintangs, the local beer. There was our other local guide who could take anything and fashion it into something. He made me a wooden hammer to break up the ground and then fashioned a shower head out of a stick of bamboo.

There were the maladies of the volunteers. All but two had their bouts of diarrhea. The first question at breakfast was always "Who has the shits today?" There were huge insects in the rain forest—spiders as big as a dinner plates and flying monsters, or so they appeared. One night, sitting under the lantern light writing in our diaries, one of the boys screamed out. Something had flown in his ear and was driving him crazy. The doctor tried to flush it out, but without the best of equipment and poor lighting, it wasn't a done deal. The buzzing stopped, but the pain continued. A few weeks later and back in civilization in Jakarta, he went to the hospital and had a huge dead black bug removed from the ear. And there was our pretty boy who dived off a rock in one of many swimming holes who chose a rock rather than the water to connect with. He split his head open just above his nose. We did a superb job of putting Humpty Dumpty back together again with Steri-strips, and it was mending beautifully without a scar. When we got him to the hospital a week later for a tetanus injection, we were horrified when the nurse removed the strips and started suturing with a big fat needle and what looked like something as heavy as a fishing line. Pretty boy probably has a big scar on his forehead to this day.

As a team, we had all bonded and all shared the same feeling of this place being the most idyllic spot and space of time we'd ever been in. None of us wanted to leave. We'd all read the book *Beaches* and could totally relate to that wanting to remain with the group in that place of beauty and peace and total contentment. But life goes on, and we moved on, first to Jakarta and then our separate ways. The funny ending for me and for what I have now experienced again and again in working together in unique places is the total separation—that group and situation were only an isolated thing in time. We all finished the project and went to Bali to enjoy a holiday on the beach before returning to wherever we were returning to. We would pass each other and say hello like it was someone we barely knew, and no one stayed in contact after that. In the kingdom, we would have risked our lives for one another and knew every aspect and behavior of each other and totally accepted one another. It's a phenomenon I shall never understand.

THE LONG TRAIN JOURNEY

I stood at the platform at the large Moscow train station with my huge backpack on and pulling a small suitcase with wheels, waiting to board the Trans-Siberian train to Beijing, feeling a bit like a fool. It was the late nineties, and I hadn't really done anything like this since hitchhiking in Europe in the late sixties. I of course was a wee bit older and should have been traveling in luxury; but no, I did still feel twenty in my head. The station was very crowded, and there were hoards of people, mainly Russians, waiting to board. I was still feeling a bit awkward and very alone.

I had just spent four days in Moscow and was still reeling with the shock of so many changes in such a short period of time. I had visited in the late seventies when I came to a seminar with a medical group from the States; it was the USSR then. Entourist, controlled by the government in those days, organized everything; and it was one of the few ways you could enter the country as a tourist. Our every movement had been controlled. It was quite difficult to go out walking on your own and go into a local pub. It was impossible to leave the city without first obtaining a visa. Every minute of every day was planned for us by Entourist, and they were most unhappy if you tried to opt out. All meals were together with the group at the hotel. To this day, I remember most the meals. It was the same for all meals each day. There was always vodka, one-liter bottle between every two to four people. There was caviar, beets, boiled eggs, always plenty of it all, and just the same each meal for the two weeks we were there.

Everything had changed. Breakfast now was just some dry toast and marmalade, an occasional boiled egg, and not-so-nice coffee. The vodka was missing as well as the caviar. The hotel was still the huge block-style building, and service did not exist; I was convinced it was the same one I had stayed in the previous visit minus the staff that couldn't do enough to satisfy. There were lots of people out on the street. Red Square looked much the same, though Lenin's tomb was not in the center with huge queues of somber-faced people waiting to view him. The big surprise was the massive GUM department store, which years earlier housed one kiosk after another of heavy cotton stockings, which now had Benetton, Next, and Lancôme. On another side of Red Square was an underground posh shopping mall, also with all designer shops. Beggars were present at all the tourist sites, subway entrances, and underground walkways. In days past, one never saw a person loitering.

There were choices now. The shops stocked a variety of goods, and gone were the bread lines. Instead of the drab, colorless clothing of years past, many young women I saw had sexy low-cut tops, and the skirts were either cut just below the panties or long with a split right up to the panties. And they had high-heeled spikes, whether working behind a desk or leading a tour group on foot. I was in pain just observing. The chain of restaurants of the West also had found Moscow.

I was intrigued by the latest of tours on offer. I spoke to a middle-aged American male while sitting in a cafe near Red Square and then suddenly he left to meet his future Russian bride. There were tour groups from Western countries, organized for the sole purpose of matching the men from these countries to Russian brides. Everything was organized for them down to the introductions. The fellow was quite content with his fiancée.

As I stood waiting to board, two women in the same age group as me wandered up and introduced themselves. They were Norwegian nurses who decided to take this journey as well before the whole world knew about the adventure. They, being Scandinavian, spoke fluent English and became frequent companions until we reached Irkutsk. They were in first-class seating, and when I needed some English-speaking company or space, it was nice to have an option.

Riding the train is a normal way of travel for the Russians, and as I chose second-class, I found myself sharing a berth with a young Russian woman and her new husband, in the military and in his full uniform. The other was a salesman from Irkutsk returning to his family after work in Moscow. He was the same age as me. Communication was going to be tough. They spoke only Russian, but the need and desire to know one another took over. Both the other woman and I discovered we spoke a bit of German. It was that and our photos and our music, my supply of vodka and their supply of food in a huge picnic basket that made us extremely good friends by the end of our five days together.

The train was old but well-maintained and spotless. Each berth contained the standard two seats across; and at night, two beds on top folded down, and the lower seats became two beds. There wasn't a lot of space. We were each given a set of linens when we boarded. There was a toilet with sink on both ends of the car stocked with toilet paper, though once it was finished, it might not appear again for a while. Each car had an attendant; ours was a very large serious Russian woman in uniform. I would have not wanted to cross her. She kept the huge samovar in the car filled with hot water for coffee or tea and cleaned the rooms each day. There was a fully stocked dining-bar car, but we had much more fun with the sharing.

The train made several stops in cities along the route. Before the train even came to a full stop, vendors came by the dozen, holding up their baskets of food, a lot homemade, drinks and trinkets, and a variety of other sundry goods. Initially, I was reluctant to try things unknown to me, but my newfound friends would buy and then give me some to taste. I came to love those stops where each might be a new culinary adventure. The things I remembered most, probably because I liked them best, were the crepes filled with cheese, the smoked fish, and fresh yogurt.

Beginning on the first night of the train journey, my berthmates took out their picnic basket from under the seat and offered me dinner. I said, "No, thanks" to be polite; I couldn't eat up their food. They were relentless in persuasion so my Stoli vodka came out. I remember with joy their faces lighting up. After that, it was a done deal. We always shared and took turns sometimes buying food from the vendors. Smoking was only permitted in the space between cars so the older guy and I would stand out there and communicate by whatever means we could.

Since it took five days to Irkutsk, there was plenty of time get to know the others in our car and passersby wandering for exercise and curiosity. The scenery was amazing once the Ural Mountains came into sight. We passed many little towns with the beautiful, delicate-looking wooden fretwork-styled houses. It was a "Dr. Zjivago" movie scene. I hated the day the train arrived in a small town before Irkutsk where the honeymooners were departing. And not much later, most departed in Irkutsk, leaving me to meet a whole new bunch of strangers. I had a couple of days in the city before boarding again for the continuation of the trip to Ulan Bator in Mongolia.

I was on my own to find my way to the hotel, but the lovely gentleman from my room on the train picked up my suitcase and walked me across all the tram tracks to the hotel. He made sure I was checked in and that the room was OK and then said his good-byes. I did manage to spend some time with the Norwegian women who were staying on a few days at Lake Baikal. I went with them and then got myself lost trying to get back to the rail station. It was difficult to get directions without Russian as one of my languages, but I made it in the nick of time.

I was now on a new train with new friends, this time a family of delightful Germans. The journey took only a day and a half. Just before the border, there was a stop for passport and customs. There were two Aussie men with whom I made a conversation. They were both writers and in the process of doing a round-the-world motorcycle journey; and for whatever reason, they were not allowed to cross with those bikes into Mongolia. They'd managed to find some Mongolians to take the bikes across, but now they had to get across themselves. I smuggled them on the train, much to the Germans' chagrin. Luckily, all passed well. What I learned from them was that this was the weekend of the annual festival of ancient sports, one being spear-throwing on horseback. People from all over the country came in, often by horse, in their traditional costumes. I couldn't believe my good fortune, and I can't tell you how much fun that was. The central square was crowded. Once again, I was in a fairy tale. What surprised me most at that time is what a modern city Ulan Bator actually was. I had visions of dirt roads, a bit like the old West, and everyone on horses. But there were high-rises, paved roads, the university, big foreign companies, but thank God, no McDonald's.

Four days there and then I returned back on the train, this time to China, and once again, new roommates. This time, they were not so pleasant, but they are embedded in my memory. I was in yet even a smaller train car with three Chinese men. They made no effort to introduce themselves or communicate. They preferred to keep the door of the room closed all the while farting to their heart's content. Besides claustrophobia, the smell was bad so I spent most of the three days outside the room. And there I met the "ugly Americans." They obviously were not on this journey for the spirit of adventure. The complaints poured forth.

We arrived at the Mongolian Chinese borders in the middle of the night and were hustled off the train, the two Americans grumbling the entire time. We had to walk a few hundred feet along the rails to the station located in a small town and wait. Meanwhile, the train was taken into a round house and lifted by cranes while the bogies (bogies being the wheels) were changed. I watched in fascination and discovered that the train tracks in the two countries were of different sizes. Rather than change trains, they changed wheels. And meanwhile, the two Americans continued to whine, "It's dangerous to be out here in the middle of the night. How dare they do this?" I stood there wondering why they traveled at all-stay home and enjoy the creature comforts. I didn't meet them again once we arrived in Beijing. I prefer the adventurers.

The next stop once the sun was up high was at a very small village, and what rose up behind it was a part of the Great Wall, unreconstructed for the tourists, without the hoards of people climbing it and without all the tourist kiosks selling T-shirts that said, "I climbed the Great Wall of China." Several hours later, we did pass the touristy part of the wall, and I shall always remember seeing the part that was magnificent.

Not long after that, we arrived in Beijing. That would be another shock to deal with. I'd been there a few years earlier, and the growth at that time was amazing. The staring didn't happen now. I used my Lonely Planet Guide to find my way. I had the latest version, and many of the streets were already replaced with construction, but China is another story.

CHINA—MOVING AS FAST AS IT CAN

My guidebook for China was the latest Fodor's Travel Guide, but it may as well have been written a century earlier. The Beijing I entered was not the same Beijing I had seen several years earlier. I followed the map in the guidebook only to find that a street with supposed historical architecture was now a new construction site. Nothing looked the same. There were huge new skyscrapers everywhere. No one stared at me, the Caucasian tourist; I was now invisible most of the time. I really did not recognize any of the Beijing I'd visited before. This was a totally new city! This was, for a time frame, several years before the Olympics, when China was a wannabe in the bid for the Olympics.

Some things in the guidebook were true; the train station was the most crowded I'd ever seen; and caring for the luggage on the way through the throngs was a real feat and definitely a reason to travel light. A guide was there to meet me, and I waited on one side of the gate, feeling abandoned while she waited on the other side, wondering if I had missed the train. When I realized I was the last one standing, I went through, and there she was. It was a relief, and she delivered me to the hotel, another surprise. It was a magnificent hotel with all the amenities, and everyone spoke English! I had stayed at the Holiday Inn the previous visit, and it was very nice, but communication was difficult then, and it was something I did not look forward to this visit. I speak a smattering of various languages, but Chinese didn't connect in my mind to anything familiar. The only hint that I was not in a four-star in the U.S. was the lack of a hair dryer, the availability of hot water at specific hours only, and the dim lighting.

I had my cold shower; luckily, it was July. Then I hit the streets; I had only a few days and wanted to miss as little as possible. The city was alive with sights and sounds and smells. I came to a square that vibrated with activity. An old woman in traditional costume was performing a dance with fans to the beat of drums. Others totally oblivious were practicing their tai chi. There were others just dancing or roller-skating. I sat at a bar across from the square and watched for hours their exuberance. I really didn't remember seeing that the previous visit. What I did remember were somber faces and suspicious looks.

I booked all the tours for the sights, even though I'd seen them before. But the best tour of all was unplanned and spontaneous. I was eating the most unusual breakfast with the dim sum and other rice and noodle dishes at a buffet restaurant when a delightful retired Chinese doctor of fifty eight years introduced himself and began chatting. The follow-up was a genuine walking tour and cultural learning experience of Beijing and of China in general, though in fact he was a doctor, not a tour guide. We walked down streets and alleyways where tourists rarely go. He showed me the courtyard homes where each family lives in one room, several families' doors opening into the same courtyard. There was only one toilet for the entire road of courtyards, and often, the residents had no options but to queue up with others and eliminate on the side of the road. I kept wondering how they could possibly be up to par to host the Olympics in a few years. We stopped for lunch at a restaurant for government employees only, near Tiananmen Square, also not on the tourist list. I was able to try several new dishes. The food was delicious and plentiful and cost all of $8 for the two of us. We had a lengthy discussion on the way of life and the impact of changes in China, and I couldn't have been more fascinated; and of course he asked me as many questions as I asked him. He told me the average doctor's salary there at that time was $400 per month. Wonder how many doctors we would have in our country if that was the case. Retirement was at age sixty; health care was free and adequate; the average age for marriage was twenty-four in the city and twenty in the rural areas; husbands and wives both work and each has their own pension. He said there were many poor living in the subway. We then parted ways, and I felt quite privileged and more informed for having met him.

I left the next morning on the train to Xian, the famous city of the terracotta army. As I gazed out the window and looked at the skyscrapers disappearing and all the tin shacks along the tracks come into view, I did think that when I returned in a week, it would probably be a new skyline, but the poor along the track would never feel the impact of the changes. Again, I was the sole woman in the compartment of four on the train but at least this time, it was air-conditioned and a bit more upmarket in its décor. I still slept in my clothes and heard the burps and farts throughout the journey. The facilities were present at each end of the car, but it is amazing that once the tissue is finished, it's never replaced, even when there are days to go. The scenery traveling north was in direct contrast to the cities. The mountains gradually appeared, and there was terraced agriculture on every bit of available usable land. There were sheep grazing, something I don't think of with China. All of the farm implements were manual, everything done by hand.

Xian was a bustling city and far more charming than Beijing. The streets were wide and tree-lined, still choked with traffic, and terrifying to cross for a Western traveler. There were many new and modern hotels. I'm sure it was due to the fame of the city since the finding of the terra-cotta soldiers. My hotel had hot water so never say anything against Xian to me. It was always busy, even at four in the morning. I lost track of the day and date, a phenomenon that always occurs when you're traveling and having fun. I made acquaintances from several different countries and frequently ran into them again when seeing the sights.

The terra-cotta army is amazing. One sees life-size soldiers stretching as far as the eye can see. The man who made the find was an elderly farmer and sat at the end, signing the pamphlets about the site. I had to wonder if he got any financial gain from the discovery. Only a week earlier, then President Clinton along with the Chinese president had visited the site, and it was still the buzz. In the evening, I attended a performance of the Tang Dynasty with someone I'd met on the tour. It was lovely to dress up and be escorted, and the performance was wonderful—a harmonious blend of ancient string instruments, mandolins, and something that sounded like a cross between a flute and a harmonica.

Then it was another day and another train, this time to Shanghai, a city of my fantasies. This time, I shared the compartment with a darling Chinese couple of substantial years like me. They spoke no English. They stared at me and smiled now and then, and I probably did exactly the same. They began sharing their morning cakes and other delicacies. I've learned never to say no and have tasted many wonderful treats, some not so wonderful, but then I know what to avoid next time. We passed through more farmland and then small towns with garbage pits along the track. I decided there was no such thing as an abandoned building in China. If it has a roof, someone lives in it. Even the old derelict train cars abandoned on tracks were occupied. The squatter toilets at each end of the train car became filthier and reeked more as each hour passed. I stopped drinking anything to avoid using them and that feeling of retching building in my throat.

Shanghai struck me as Hong Kong with a Manhattan style and a lot wealthier than Beijing. There were hoards of people shopping in the many malls, and the choices were as many as in most Western countries. And of course, there was the "Hard Rock Café," which was expensive and jumping. I hate to admit it, but every now and then, a mild feeling of homesickness occurs, and I give in and have a burger. I promise it's not more than once a month.

Somewhere along the route, a young Chinese man latched on and offered his services as a tour guide. I thanked him and said no, but he refused to leave my side, pointing out places and giving information as we went. He helped me buy a camera (mine had packed up) though I was quite capable of doing so, and I remained annoyed with that purchase until my next camera a couple of years later. I understood very little of what he said secondary to his accent and so I became more and more annoyed. I went to a tea house, and he followed me right in and sat down so I bought him tea while I pondered how to get rid of him. He had a horrible-sounding cough, and I kept thinking he probably had tuberculosis. He constantly grabbed my arm as we walked to get my attention. I finally walked back to my safe haven—the Hard Rock (an exception to the once-a-month rule) and said good-bye. He asked for the fee for his services, and my chin dragged on the road. I've never known how to handle that one well. I gave him a small amount of change, breathed a sigh of relief, and went inside.

It was back to Beijing after that and then on to Thailand. China was fascinating; and several years later while working in Australia, I applied for a job in Shanghai. I didn't get it, but I'm sure if I had gone back, it would have been yet a different country.

BACKPACKING MAMA

Up until I flew into Bangkok from Beijing, I say I was backpacking, but what I really was doing was carrying a backpack rather than a suitcase. Everything had been planned through a travel agent friend and so I knew where I was going and where I was staying each night. The hotel rooms were always at least two stars with some amenities. There is security in knowing that a charming unique chamber awaited me at the end of each traveling day. I arrived in Bangkok a bit nervous about how to proceed on my own and quite ill with fever and gastrointestinal symptoms and a horrific cough. I was sure I had picked up tuberculosis from the man in Shanghai who coughed continuously and then kept touching me. Of course, rationally, I knew it wasn't good but I felt I wanted to die so rather than find a backpacker's hotel, I booked myself into the Marriot Hotel and enjoyed all the comforts for a few days. I pretended I had plenty of money and went to the elaborate and expensive buffet at the Oriental Hotel that had been recommended as well as a few other places, in style. I just totally pampered myself for the next week and probably spent more money than I would in a month after that. It's a good thing because the big change was about to occur. The real backpacking began, and I did need to mind what I was spending.

I booked the train to Cheng Mai in the north in the first-class cabin per recommendation of my guidebook; it's very cheap traveling on trains in developing countries, and first-class is oh so much more civil. My cabinmate was a Dutch woman fifteen years my junior, a teacher and a seasoned traveler. We bonded during the journey, and she became my teacher in the art of backpacking. I had booked a two-star hotel recommended by the Lonely Planet Guide, but talking to Anne, I realized I could travel much cheaper and longer if I trailed her, and so I did. I moved over to a$3 room in the same little hotel that she was staying. It was a far down cry from the hotel I had booked and, compared to the Marriot, a gutter, but hey, it was only a bed for the night. The rest of the time we were out exploring and experiencing the culture. The room was the size of my bathroom back home and had cracked plaster walls, no window, an overhead rickety fan, and a twin bed; and it was dirty. That was it, but the sheets were clean, and there was a functioning cold shower shared by all at the end of the hall. It sufficed once I got over the shock of the change. And just to note, cold showers are a blessing in those hot, humid climates.

I signed up for a Thai cooking class, and Anne went diving—that was her love. We booked a three-day excursion to Cheng Rai near the Burmese border. There was a group of a dozen others from several countries around the world, all in their twenties, and our guide, Chai. The first day was an eleven-kilometer trek up the hills to the small border villages in intense July heat. My legs turned to jelly the last kilometer, and once again, I prayed for survival. The others, being younger, acted tough but also collapsed for a while once we reached our open hut for the night. There were no facilities in terms of bathing so we just remained reeking of sweat, but at least it was the lot of us. Chai prepared the local food and was a wonderful storyteller. We all shared a conversation. After that, we were offered opium to smoke by the locals. The guidebooks warn against partaking, but most did have some, and some enjoyed the experience more than others. I remained a prude. It's one of those few things over which I will not break rules when traveling. I've seen the consequences when someone is caught, and in foreign countries, it can be extremely severe, at least in this time period, it still was. The second day, we trekked to yet another village along the border where the Burmese tribes are still in traditional colorful dress, selling their beads and souvenirs to the tourists trekking through. I did a bit of cursing at the guide for the uphill trek since I had not been forewarned and laughed later. It's like having a baby—once it's over, you forget the pain of it. We followed on with an elephant ride to another village, and once off the elephants, another trek in the searing heat to yet another village. There we stayed in a new hut, completed that very day near a very welcoming river. It was bliss except for the mosquitoes. The next day, we all piled onto bamboo rafts going through the jungle and over small rapids with idyllic scenery the entire way back to Cheng Mai.

Anne was going to Phoket next for more scuba diving, and I thought, *Why not?* On the plane, we chose a hotel at Karon Beach at $5 a night per person, which sounded very nice for the price. And it was as lovely as described. The rooms were large, bleached white, open, and airy. There was an attached bathroom, and we each had a double bed. It was a short walking distance to the center of the town and a short taxi ride to Patong, the larger town with all the night life. The hotel itself had a large open restaurant/bar at the entrance. There was a massage parlor next door and lots of movement in the corridors of our hotel throughout the night. We didn't pay much attention to it until we also noticed that in the early morning, when we went for breakfast, couples were sitting regularly at the bar looking like they'd had a very rough night. We learned several days later that it was a hotel for prostitution and that it was fairly common in Asian and African countries for the cheaper hotels to serve both backpackers and prostitutes. It was a practice I had forgotten until I ran into it again in Africa. Oh, well, why not? As long as the rooms are clean and the walls are thick.

Anne left after this for another diving tour and then the return to Holland. I had no restrictions, so I continued on to Penang, Malaysia, by local bus. That was arduous. The bus was a van and held approximately twelve people. Every seat was filled, and there was no room for luggage, so it's under your feet or on your lap. It's why backpackers travel light. I shed things wherever I could and learned to travel much lighter. This ride was a full-day traveling over hot dusty bumpy roads in a vehicle without air-con, and then we had to change vans on three different occasions. The last driver was a Chinese Malaysian, who wanted to discuss Clinton politics with me as we crossed the border into Malaysia. After twelve hours in the van, I think I may have been rude in my response. I just wanted a decent room and a cold shower.

Penang initially looked more prosperous than the towns and villages we had passed in Thailand; there appeared to be better roads, more landscaping, and nicer homes. But as time went on and I walked the streets, it all became a oneness. This was Asia, and I was in an Asian city with a style quite distinct from Europe or the U.S. The old hotel popular with backpackers looked grand and ornate from the outside, but once inside, it was extremely basic. But it was friendly and had a common area where travelers could sit comfortably and share their experiences as well as make recommendations. I often choose to backpack rather than stay in a nice hotel when I travel alone. Not only is it cheap, but also it is far more social. Amongst backpackers and travelers, age is not an issue: the commonality is the love of travel, and friendships are made easily regardless of age or nationality. I hiked up the Penang Hill and met a lovely young Austrian couple who were attempting to find the trail, as was I. We hiked together, discussing politics, religion, psychology, and who knows what else. On the descent, we stopped at a food stand to eat and have a beer. We met for dinner again the next evening and then parted for our next destination, although we did talk about meeting again in Kuala Lumpur. I love that, and it only seems to happen when I backpack rather than travel in style and, it's what I love most about traveling; I enjoy the architecture and museums, but the people really define culture.

Then it happened, I had very little cash left. I went to eat at a place which appeared to be a British pub and had the Visa sign posted on the outside. I asked if they did indeed take credit cards and was assured they did. I had a full meal, not knowing when the next would be, and when I took out the credit card, the answer was no. This does happen consistently in developing countries, the moral being that one must always be ahead in the cash department. It was a struggle to find the one bank that would give money on the credit card, and it was a half-day process. ATMs can be difficult to find as well, and often in developing countries, one can try many before finding one that will accept a specific card. The restaurant trusted me to return the next day with the cash to pay for the meal; there's the negative and then the positive.

It was time to move on and the next stop was Malacca, in the South. This time it was an overnight air-conditioned bus, and I thought I would be found frozen to death in the back of the bus after it arrived at our destination. I found a guesthouse in the center of the charming pink town with Dutch history and architecture. Once again, it was charming on the outside and left a lot to be desired on the inside. I had a room with no windows, a bed with no cover sheet, and a fan. The monsoon rains came, and the street filled up with over a foot of water in a few hours. There were no sidewalks so it was a trick to get in and out of the house and to walk through the dirty water, not knowing what was under the surface. One day was quite enough to see the sights and take a river boat tour to see the native trees and crocodile-sized lizards. I was now ready for the big city of Kuala Lumpur.

I arrived by bus in the wee hours of the morning, and getting used to the traffic, noises, and multitudes of people took a few minutes. The city is large with many new building and shopping centers. There are the Hard Rock Cafés and Starbucks, and a few streets over, the markets and local restaurants in the street. Malaysian food is hot and spicy and delicious, and when you sit in the street to eat, you of course also breathe in the fumes of the automobiles. I spent many hours there taking in the ambience and life of the city and sucking in carbon monoxide. I walked a thousand miles, or so it felt, seeing all the sights. Malaysia is a mix of Malay, Indian, and Chinese, a real melting pot, though Islam predominates in terms of religion. The heads are covered, and the mosques are plenty. The people are welcoming and accepting of differences. I spent several days there and met many people with whom I sat and chatted. One young Australian had just returned from Sarawak, which was a part of what was Borneo, and had nothing but good to share so instead of moving on to Australia next, I went to Borneo, another place of my fantasies.

Before I left I visited the Batu Caves, which bear mentioning; and though I don't treasure sights as much as the people and culture, it wouldn't have been complete without seeing the caves. They are a historical Hindu religious sight, in fact the most sacred Hindu shrine outside of India. There is art on all the walls as well as the usual monkeys everywhere. It is known in particular for the annual Thaipusam festival held in the early months of each year. Pilgrims come from around the world. There is a procession up a two-hundred-seventy-two-step stairway to the caves. Some of the men have a carrier called a *kavadi* on their shoulders to which are attached skewers which pierce the skin on their backs. With this, they pull very heavy offerings to the gods, pulling the weight up against gravity and through the masses of people attending.

And so it was on to Kuching, Sarawak, and the Grand Continental Hotel, I felt in my element again, and it really didn't cost much more than a backpacker's in Australia. It's a lovely city and far less demanding than are many. Most tourists don't make it this far unless they're interested in the natural habitat of the orangutans. It was one of the reasons I came, and the other was the long canoes through the jungle to stay in the well-known long houses where tourists were once forbidden and head-hunting was a way of life.

The trip to the longhouses was money well spent, and I was thrilled to see the area now before tourism and modernization totally destroyed it. I made instant friends with two professional British men, both with incredible senses of humor, and so we shared our perceptions, a lot of laughs, and a lot of beers. We arrived at the jetty to our first disappointment. The long canoes had a motor at the back. It was an hour on the Lemonak River through magnificent rain forest with the overhanging trees to our second slight disappointment. The original longhouse had a second guest house, new, next to it. We had proper beds with mosquito nets, showers, flush toilets, and lights—so much for real adventure. We were allowed to walk through the original longhouse, with restrictions, and the dried human heads were hanging on that side.

In the evening, a reception was held in the original longhouse. It started with a meal of traditional food then rice wine. We came bearing gifts of biscuits and cigarettes (an expectation) followed by traditional dancing, in which we were fully expected to partake and did after enough of the rice wine. Of course, the evening ended with all of the villagers bringing in their handmade wares for purchase. There were baskets, mats, blowguns, ironwood carvings and jewelry, no desiccated heads. We all made purchases. How could you not? And my treasure was a fertility god carved from ironwood for $4. Some will be horrified, but in the morning, our last bit of entertainment included a cockfight and a blowgun demonstration. I suppose that the cockfight is slightly more civil than headhunting as a hobby.

Then it was a return to Kuching once again on the river. I did hate parting with my newfound friends, but such is the life of a backpacker. There are the wonderful friends you meet and also the not-so-wonderful, in fact the downright obnoxious; and you just have to remember it as part of your experience and your learning. I returned to Kuching to have an Indian man I had met before leaving for the jungle awaiting me. He was probably twenty years my junior, and I told him so but nonetheless, we'd made an appointment to meet. I was not looking forward to it; but still not wanting to hurt anyone's feelings and accepting it as a cultural experience, I met him as promised. An experience it was, though not exactly as I had anticipated or desired. His conversation immediately led to his desire to make love, if that's what you can call it. In trying not to offend, I attempted to divert, but he kept revisiting the same topic. I next learned of his sexual habits like he enjoyed masturbating at least four times a day, and he measured his penis because he truly believed that women were concerned with size—way too much information—and at that point, it really was my obligation to tell him he was inappropriate and walk away. And I did—offensive or not.

The flight for Sydney was the next day, none too soon, and there the search for kangaroos would begin. By this point, and almost six months after beginning my journey, I wanted familiarity and at least a culture that was a bit more like my own.

In Search of Kangaroos

I went to Australia in search of kangaroos, and I found the Garden of Eden. I didn't find the kangaroos right away, but I found the wallabies, and between you and me, I can't tell the difference. I woke up one morning to a flock of turkeys in my front garden and a mob of wallabies in back of the house. I opened the back door, and they lifted their heads up from the grass and stood tall, just staring at me. The little joeys hopped back in mums' pouches, preparing for impending danger. But I just stood and stared in wonder. I used to stare at the deer and elk on my property in Colorado, but they were so sensitive they moved at the blink of an eye, literally. I much prefer the wallabies; it's like they're daring me to move forward, and we'll stare at each other for a few minutes. When I go back inside, they would lean forward and start eating the grass again.

The outbackers who have lived here awhile laughed at my awe of the creatures. They say they're just a nuisance. They hop in front of cars and become road kill, never mind the damage to the vehicle. They hop fences, often destroying them as they do. They get on the runways of the small outback airports and graze, only looking up and staring at the approaching Cessna so the planes have "to do a scare the wallaby run" before they actually take off. Wallaby meat in the prop of a plane doesn't help its flying. They're still magnificent creatures to anyone but a native Australian. In any other place in the world, one only sees them in a zoo.

I went to all the places more familiar to the tourists first. Sydney, with its trademark opera house, is the New York or London of Australia. People move about very quickly without looking at anyone directly. The dominant color of dress is black and charcoal, and they scurry to their offices or lunch or a trendy cocktail bar in the late afternoon. I moved on to Melbourne, the San Francisco of Australia. And so it was, a lovely Victorian city with lots of cafés and bars and places to hear music, a wonderful cultural center, parks, and even trams. I loved both cities, but the burning question for me was still what made this country unique and why I always had this intense desire to come here and stay for a while, halfway around the world from my family and friends.

I came to Australia to find a job, not the easiest thing to do if you're an American. I don't begrudge that, we don't make it easy for Australians in the States. I was told by a woman in immigration that the only way I'd be allowed to stay was to marry an Australian. As I hadn't met one who popped the question, I searched for other options; and it came in the form of an advertisement in the Melbourne newspaper for remote nurses in the Northern Territory. I made the telephone inquiry, and they were willing to do a work-sponsorship visa. The rest is history.

I hopped on a Greyhound bus and made my way from Melbourne through Adelaide then North passing through Coober Pedy, Ayers Rock, King's Canyon, Alice Springs, Tennant Creek, Katherine, and finally Darwin. Each mile I traveled north, I saw more of the Australia I had fantasized for years. The vast distances of Australia came into being. We pressed North on the Stuart Highway, a single-lane straight road, for endless hours, passing an occasional road train or car. They became fewer and father in between the further North we went, until we reached Katherine. Mountain ranges were visible in the distance in the center around Alice Springs. The plains were covered with short trees, Spinifex and, after Alice, termite mounds up to six-foot tall. There were occasional roadside houses for sustenance and fuel, not the modern new Shell complex, but very old pub-style buildings, showing their age through the history on the walls-old photos, graffiti, and memorabilia. I'd found the Australia I'd been searching for.

I reached Darwin in December, the wet season. The North is tropical. There are two seasons, the wet and the dry. The wet begins with a hot, sunny sky. It's very humid, so much so that one wants a shower every hour, and even after the shower, one never feels dry. It's great for the skin, no moisturizer necessary. The skin can't possibly age. Early in the afternoon, the sky clouds over and becomes darker with brilliant hues of pink and purple from the sun behind the clouds. Suddenly, the monsoon rains come. It's like someone has turned a tank of water and poured it over you full force, and it can last anywhere from fifteen minutes to a few hours. It seemed, more often than not, the skies cleared before dark, and there was an incredible sunset over the seas surrounding Darwin. I've never seen such beautiful sunsets anywhere. It makes up for the lost sweat and misery of the day.

Darwin is a small city as cities go. It was attacked during World War II and almost totally destroyed by Cyclone Tracy in the seventies. Because of its proximity to Asia, Asian influence is present, though not in its architecture. It's a laid-back city, creating the ever-present feeling of being on vacation. It comes alive after dark. Dressing up for the evening means wearing a clean lightweight sexy top and jeans or trousers and wearing makeup and perfume. Evening entertainment is restaurants, bars, and cinema in the wet season. I said when I left for the outback and my job that I would need a liver transplant if I had stayed in Darwin any longer. It's friendly and international, and I loved going there on my weekends off work.

Darwin is one of the gates to the outback and the uniqueness of Australia. The Northern Territory is a territory and not a state and in that sense resembles the Wild West, which unfortunately no longer exists in the States. It's a place of lots of space and not lots of people, but the quality of relationships has not been ruined yet by materialism. Time is spent just getting together without the one-upmanship of Western society. A get-together involves the kids running around, screaming, the old folks sitting around, quietly observing, and the ones in the middle chatting lively and putting down the occasional (?) beer. There doesn't seem to be the boundaries of worker not socializing with the boss or even the minister of the government. It's just one big happy, sometimes crazy, function.

Timber Creek was the community to which I was sent. It's one of many creeks—Pine Creek, Halls Creek, and Tennant Creek. It's on the Victoria Highway halfway between Katherine and Kununnura in Western Australia, two hundred miles to either place; and there's nothing in terms of a stop in-between. The mail arrives by Greyhound bus three times a week. There were a couple of small shops attached to gas stations-cum-pubs-cum-motels-cum-caravan parks. There was a small dirt airstrip used by charter planes for medical emergencies and the weekly visit from the doctor and in the dry-tourist season tours over the Kimberley. There was a new school for the approximately thirty white and Aboriginal children up to the age of twelve. After that, they board in the city or attend School of the Air. There's a new modern medical clinic, which provides care to both the white and Aboriginal population of three hundred and to the outlying Aboriginal communities. Some of these in the wet season can only be reached at times by aircraft. There is also a police station and holding unit, mostly for out-of-control drunks, and there's a large forest ranger group because there are several entrances to Gregory National Park in the area. But there is far more to the Timber Creek area than that, and it's why I call it my Garden of Eden.

It is a core place for nature. I'm not saying it's the only one; it's the one I discovered for myself. I woke each day to the sound of birds—cockatiels the size of large parrots covering an entire tree, miniature parrots in bright red and chartreuse, kookaburras doing their very noisy speeches, guhlas in their light grey and reds. It's only a few of the varieties. In the nearby Victoria River, a fisherman's paradise, for the barramundi, crocodiles waited for the next meal, which could be an inattentive pet dog or cow or human, though they seem to prefer the animals, thank God. It is necessary to be on guard, though. Going down the river in a boat, I've seen as many as twenty lying on the bank, sunning themselves. The most known is about twelve to fifteen feet in length. There are also the shier creatures that swiftly move away into the tall grass snakes of the most poisonous types and goannas, the most beautiful being the frilled-neck lizard that fans out a collar around its head when startled. Another of my favorites is the little bright chartreuse green frog that manages to be everywhere—in the sink when you're ready to brush your teeth or in the toilet as you get ready to sit on the throne. Insects of every kind are in abundance and, though fearful-looking, really don't like us any better than we like them. The only exceptions are the pesky sweat flies and sand flies. The sweat flies, in particular, swarm about the nose, eyes, and mouth for that tiny droplet of moisture. Hence the joke is that the Aussie salute is the hand waving back and forth across the front of the face.

When I first came out, I was often asked by friends if I was bored living in the bush. After all, I was a city girl and very involved in the social scene. I did not find boredom to be an issue in the bush; in fact, the days went so quickly. I thirsted for more hours in each day. I spent a lot of every day meditating on the nature that surrounded me. Escarpment was all around. In the wet season, waterfalls come down and created swimming holes, a welcome relief during and after the heat of the day. There are little walking trails everywhere, safer used in pairs in case a snake is caught unaware. The boab tree is known only in the Territory though similar to a tree in Africa. It is shaped like a huge grey bottle with a clump of unruly green hair on the top. The sky is a deep blue, the ground is a deep red; and the contrast continues to keep me in awe. The sunsets are different than Darwin but equally gorgeous. As the sun goes down, the escarpment increases in an intense red color, almost as if it is on fire. Once the sun is behind it, hues of purple and pink color the sky.

Aside from the beauty, activity abounds. There was a community center where there were regular "barbees" (slang for barbeque) and weekly volleyball. There was a tennis court, a playing field, and a horse track. Anyone interested in riding could come each Saturday, round up a horse, and ride. Afterward, everyone socialized and brought food for a barbeque. The school provided a "barbee" each Friday at lunchtime as a fund-raiser. Available community members attended and watched the children receive their achievement awards for the week. The highlight for the school was the annual twilight dinner put on by the children for the community. The kids prepared and served a four-course meal to those who attended. Everyone took off their casual clothes for a day and came dressed to the nines. The other large annual event was the September horse races. People came from far and wide for the event. The Territory encompassed many large cattle stations, and horses and rodeos are a part of the lifestyle.

Loving my job was a part of the total bliss of living in Eden. After all, during one's working years, more time is spent doing that than anything else but sleeping. In the Territory, I found a nursing job that some nurses only fantasize about. It was as a remote nurse, and there were many days I felt as though I was in a movie scene. We worked out of a clinic but are certainly were not enclosed within four walls. There were scalped heads from boomerangs, stabbing from drunken brawls, horrendous collisions because at that time there was no speed limit on the main highway. I even made international news for a crocodile bite I treated on an eight-year-old Aboriginal girl. As was true anywhere, it was difficult to recruit doctors for remote areas so the clinics were and probably still are managed by nurses and Aboriginal health workers. The doctors visited on a weekly or every-other-week basis, and a medical plane was flown out with an Air Med team to evacuate emergencies, but that can take several hours so stabilization was done in the clinic. Sometimes people died who may not have had they been in a hospital with equipment nearer at hand, but it is a choice made when living or traveling in the outback.

Treatment of illness, assessment, preventative care, teaching, emergency care, and providing necessary care were all a part of the role. We treated within the community, and we went out to more remote Aboriginal communities one or two days a week to provide the same service. We flew in a Cessna every other week during the wet season to one of the communities that would have been more than a two-hour drive on a dirt track. Every time I got on that plane, I used to think, "Most people pay to fly on these things, and I'm being paid." The old folks were always lined up waiting for their medication and checkup. The women and children would line up next. It was the rule of the community. The children often had scabies or boils to be treated. The children would run around the clinic with snotty noses; and between treating folks, we wiped snotty noses. The women came for their annual women's check with a bit of pushing. They tended to be shy and not make eye contact. In general, the women wanted to be treated by women, and the men by men. The men tended to be less compliant with medical care, and we saw fewer other than for treatment of injuries.

The Aboriginals were secretive about many aspects of their culture, and I think if I had stayed twenty years, as an outsider, I still could not claim to be an expert. The Westernization was to varying degrees dependent upon the remoteness. I heard terms like "dreamtime," "woman's business," "men's business," "sorry business," "payback," and it did influence the kinds of things I had to treat, but I didn't totally understand what all of that was about. I know that in some places, tribal circumcision was still performed, and sometimes, we had to treat the complications. Payback may be a spear through someone's torso or a head wound from an axe or club, and I might have to treat that. Local medicine was often used first, and then we might see the person several days after the injury.

Other things more unique here were the treatment of snakebites, box jellyfish stings, spider bites, and tropical diseases. They didn't occur often, but it's not something you would even expect to see in a clinic in Denver or San Francisco. Another interesting one was removing fish barbs out of faces, backs, arms, legs, you name it. Whenever I was on call, I didn't have a clue what would come through that clinic door. I waited in anticipation or dread. I wasn't sure which at times. More often than not, it was a minor cut or the flu, and I would breathe a sigh of relief.

And so the search for kangaroos led me to that place. I can't think of anywhere more beautiful, more awe-inspiring, and more of an adventure.

DILI DREAMING

I have been known for sometime not doing enough research prior to going to a country and therefore not being totally prepared for any eventuality. My weekend to Dili in East Timor just after the country's independence in 2002 was one of those. I worked remote outside of Darwin and normally went to Darwin to play on my weekends off. I suddenly had one of those sitting-on-the-toilet whims and decided to visit East Timor on the next weekend off. After all, it was a country that I had not yet seen. Secondly, I had never visited a war-torn country. And thirdly, it was only a bit over an hour over the sea. If you say that's insanity, you wouldn't be alone in thinking that, and when I look at that now, eight years later, surely I must have been having a brain-damaged moment.

I arrived in Darwin just before Christmas in 1998. East Timor was a news item on a daily basis. The Indonesian occupation had occurred in 1975, and during that time, there was conflict, huge death tolls, and no infrastructure remaining. There was a referendum for independence in 1999, and anti-independence militias, supported by Indonesia, moved in pushing refugees in massive numbers to West Timor. Most of the major players were afraid to destroy their relations with Indonesia, but after the militias came, INTERFET was created and Australia in particular became involved. Darwin, as the nearest city and major port, became a beehive of activity. There were military who came and UN workers in mass numbers taking their R&R in Darwin. It was the nearest wild and crazy city in the developed world. The hotels, bars, and restaurants were filled on the weekend with people often from the UN, throwing around their money.

Friends I either knew or worked with went over to Dili to assist medically or otherwise. One friend took a job as a chef in the hotel in Dili that was housing many of the UN workers. Some returned with malaria or dengue fever, unknown in Australia, and there was awareness of prevention so that it would not become a problem. Planes flew on at least a daily basis back and forth between Darwin and Dili. Independence came a year later.

It was after that when I got the bug to visit and booked a ticket. The travel agent I had used regularly was a bit surprised and did warn me that there was no travel insurance available, including medical, but did with some difficulty find me a hotel. There was little other information. The only thing I knew was that taxis were available at the airport and that I might be able to find my chef friend because there weren't that many good hotels in operation.

I flew out in the late afternoon on a Friday and arrived in Dili at sunset. The first thing I noticed was that aside from the Ansett (since bankrupt) plane that I flew over in, the tarmac was covered with the big gray UN planes. Many were cargos. The airport was tiny without any frills. The only others on the plane I was on were aid workers and businessmen or diplomats. No, indeed, it wasn't yet a tourist destination. The queue moved slowly and orderly, and there were no hassles coming through passport control and customs. I came through to the other side, and indeed there were taxis. Amen, no problems now.

Well, that wasn't exactly true because I gave the name of the hotel to the taxi driver, and it was not familiar to him. I then presented him with the printout from the travel agent with the address. He went to the address, and there was only a small outdoor food stand at that location. He stopped many times and asked local people and other taxi drivers. No one knew of any such hotel. He did a lot of driving to various areas of the city without any satisfaction. I was beginning to get a bit edgy myself at that point. Luckily, I had not made a deposit for the hotel and I could sense his frustration so I took out my Lonely Planet Bible, most likely outdated, and gave him a name out of that. He was quite happy to deposit me at the gate, take his fare, and say good-bye.

I had chosen a hotel that had been listed as charming, colonial style, and the most popular in Dili, and it was on the main road in and walking distance to the center. What I didn't take into account was the fact that this was immediate post-conflict or probably at that time in my experience, I had no idea what post-conflict meant. The hotel was extremely basic with no frills whatsoever, though you could fantasize that it might have been quite lovely at some point in the past. It presented itself as a backpacker's hostel, and they had one remaining available room at $150 Australian, only a bit less than the American dollar. Initially in shock, I did come to the realization I had no other choice. In post-conflict countries, where there is limited everything, they can charge what they want; and the locals see the UN workers in particular with big money to spend. The room had only a cot bed, a dribble for a shower, and only limited generator-powered electricity. I learned that the hotel where my friend worked was walking distance on the same street but decided against walking over there to find him at night. It was dark without street lamps, and at least I had the common sense to suspect it probably was quite dangerous after dark.

Things looked much better in the morning, and I went in search of my friend. I found the hotel which was of a far higher standard than the one in which I was staying. It had a lovely garden behind bamboo walls with a bar and restaurant, and the staff was extremely amicable. So I became quite friendly with all the staff while waiting for my friend. I had not told my friend I was coming since at that time there was limited communication access, but he didn't chase me away. Rather, I think he was thrilled to see a familiar face and immediately began organizing around his work hours. The hotel staff was happy to oblige us and allowed me to stay in a worker's room that was away in Darwin that weekend. The friend was allowed to use one of the hotel's service trucks to show me around.

Dili was street after street of shells of houses and buildings with weed growth all around. The roads were potholed. UN vehicles were in abundance, and many in uniforms were armed. In the midst of what remained of the business area, there was a two-story building, the second story a shell, but on the first story was a Western-style patisserie where mainly expats wiled away free time and met with other expats. It stood out in the rubble, but a sight I've seen in every post-conflict country I've worked in since. It's a small oasis in the desert for expats and the wealthy locals remaining because no one else could afford a cup of coffee there. The coffee cost more than what many earn in a day's work.

In the evening, we went to the only real disco that was open and hopping in Dili. It was frequented by the expats and locals and, up until the night that we went, had no cover charge. It was a large tropical-style building, pleasant enough and by nine in the evening, filled with people drinking and dancing. There was some drunkenness but no fights or outrageous behavior. A few hours after we arrived, there was a thunderous noise on the outside of the building. It sounded as though something was striking the building and went on for ten minutes. We heard sirens in the distance, but no one else seemed disturbed so we carried on dancing. We stayed for at least another hour after that and then proceeded to leave. We walked out the exit to see the building surrounded by UN vehicles and uniformed men standing with guns pointed.

I didn't know whether to run as fast as I could or duck back into the building. We chose to walk quickly back to our vehicle and get the hell out of there. We later learned that that the locals were extremely angry that a cover charge had been imposed because again it was more than they made in a day and now basically only expats could afford to enter. The cover charge had been imposed because more and more, there was fighting and rivalry between the expat and local males over the local woman. I guess the expats won. Is this not just another way in which we create hostilities and bad feelings in the countries we say we are helping?

We saw another example of the same sort of thing the next day. We drove along the beach toward the outskirts of the city. It's what the locals seemed to do with their families as well. The roads and walkways were filled with people, and it had that Sunday kind of feeling. There were hand-pulled wheeled vending carts in the center of the road selling candies, chewing gum, cigarettes, and other sundry items. People would drive next to the cart to make their purchase, and we did the same. The vehicle behind us started honking its horn and then suddenly revved the engine. We turned to see one of the UN land cruisers. They sped past us, shouting, "You're just like the damn natives." It's that kind of behavior that sets me off. They are the guests in the country whether they are visitors or are in a helping capacity. It's the sort of thing that got us called "the ugly Americans" years earlier. Now there's a lot more ugly than just Americans. I'm sure we spent the next hour ranting and raving while driving.

The coastline was beautiful, and I remember thinking, *So much more so than Bali, which is the beach resort destination that Aussies frequent for holidays.* I could see that as a holiday destination within ten years, once the country was stabilized and the infrastructure up and running again. And after that beach drive, it was time to return to the airport and return to Darwin. It was harder reentering Darwin than it was to enter East Timor. I did have a long-term visa for my employment there, so normally, there were no problems. This particular time, the agent at the passport window asked the usual question, "What were you doing in Dili?" I responded with "Just there for a weekend holiday." And her response to me reverberated across the entire room. "Holiday? In Dili?" She did allow me reentry after a few more questions.

That was eight years ago. Today, the country's security still remains fragile. There were outbreaks of violence again in 2006 and 2008. There are continued underlying tensions over control of oil in the waters between Australia and East Timor. Crime rates are high, and gang-related violence and robberies are a common occurrence. Infrastructure is still not good, medical care often requires a trip over to Darwin. I think my ten-year prediction for East Timor for a tourist destination fell a bit short. But I think I'm happy that I saw it as it was then and not in the future when the beaches are packed with a million tourists from everywhere and there's not a local to be seen other than the ones selling beads, braiding hair, and giving massages.

A Country of Don'ts
Rather than Dos

I was still working in Australia after five years, but the challenge was no longer there and my feet were itching again. There was no rush, I started reading the "Nursing Journal" ads on a weekly basis for jobs in more exotic places and applied for a few. I applied and interviewed for a position in Shanghai, which sounded very interesting but someone else was chosen. There were lots of positions in Saudi Arabia, and it was a place of interest for me. The Middle East would be new territory, the money was good, and there were so many countries in the Middle East that would be easily accessible for travel. I applied for a midwife position and was offered a management position in Home Health care where I was far more experienced. I made the decision quickly, had a few months break with my family, and then left for Riyadh.

People go to work in Saudi from almost every country in the world for many different reasons, the primary reason being big money which is tax free. Others come to learn more about Islam and experience the ultimate Islamic country, to work in the country where Mecca is located and therefore afford the once-in-a-lifetime mandatory pilgrimage if Muslim. Others come simply to experience living and working in a Middle Eastern country, or some more personally to get off of alcohol or drugs because that is totally forbidden. Finally others come to escape some situation back in their homeland whether it be child support, a crime or a husband or wife no longer loved. I met many in each of these categories.

Saudi is not a country open to visitors and unless you work in the country or enter the country on business with a special visa, you will never see it. The exception for all Muslims is that they may attend Hajj, which is the annual pilgrimage for Muslims around the world. One sees Saudis everywhere in the world, the woman in their black abayas and total head cover, only the eyes showing, and the men in their flowing white dresses with a checkered red and white tablecloth wrapped around their head. They are normally perceived as being extremely wealthy and powerful. Within the country, the aloofness prevails, and there is no deviation from the dress code, but poverty is present. The rich are very rich and often have some ties to the royal family, and the poor are often very poor and have no ties. Beggars are occasionally seen on the streets.

Riyadh is a large city with eight million inhabitants and growing. It is glowing with neon lights, and many streets are lined with neon palm trees. That was an enigma to me—why neon palms when you can have the real things. There are very large modern shopping centers with all of the trendy name shops everywhere in the city. It's what the Saudis do besides go to the mosques because almost everything else is forbidden. The architectural style of the buildings is way out there. Each building put up has to be more magnificent and unique than the last.

The main roads are four and five lanes on each side, always packed with cars. You see cars packed with children bouncing up and down—no seatbelts (we used to call them human missiles), cars weaving back and forth, and others turning to the left from the right-hand lane at stop signs. I never did learn if there were rules of the road. It seemed to be the one place where there were no don'ts. I was happy that I wasn't allowed to drive there and frequently closed my eyes while a passenger. There was every super or hypermarket from any country you've been to. Starbucks and any other restaurant chain from around the world can be found. There are several golf courses, well-maintained behind the walls of either compounds or hotels. Riyadh is the seat of the government for Saudi Arabia and hosts all the embassies and consulates. It is one of the New Yorks of the Middle East.

But with all its glitz and glamour, Saudi Arabia is a country of challenges and especially for a Westerner because the country is the most fundamentalist of Muslim countries and rules are expected to be strictly adhered to. And there are many more rules for women, and for a Western woman, it is extremely prohibiting. I was asked the question by many," Are you out of your mind? Why would you go and risk doing something inadvertently and then end up being stoned?" The oil company in earlier years interviewed the wife along with the husband with job interviewees to assess whether or not she would be able to adapt before hiring that person. If you're a woman, you must wear the abaya—all black so the woman can bake in the desert sun. Best to put on the black head scarf as well. Even though the king says it's not necessary for the Westerners, the religious police will chase you down the corridors shouting in English at the top of their lung capacity, "Cover your head, woman!" and they do have power. A woman cannot drive so she finds a taxi driver she can trust (usually available through the place of employment) to take her wherever she wants to go and get her home safely. Of course, if there's an accident while she's in the taxi, it is her fault. She's a woman and a temptress after all, and the driver would not have had an accident if she hadn't been in the car to distract him. And of course, no photography is allowed. I know of a couple of cases where people were sent immediately back to their countries of origin after snapping a photo, never being allowed to return. All my photos were from the inside of a bus or on excursions to sights, the only exception.

Most things are illegal such as cinema, but if you have a TV, you can see just about anything you want, lurid sex included. Any religion other than Islam, pure and simple, does not exist. You are a Muslim if you enter Saudi except you can't go into Mecca unless you're a real Muslim. The list goes on. Women cannot sit in Starbucks. Did you know coffee can be drunk in public only by men? The women must hide behind screens. A woman and man should not be seen alone together unless they are married, and they best have the papers along to prove it. At one point, a friend was going to have her son come to visit, but the hoops she would have had to jump through to make that happen seemed too much to deal with.

So the trick in Saudi is to know the don'ts and know them well, and the challenge is learning to break them without getting caught. Everything can be had and done in Saudi; it's simply a matter of knowing where it is, how to get there, and to practice discretion at all times. It's a big game. The expat community is well-established, and there are a multitude of expats who have been there for more than several years. Like starting in school, the older ones help the newer ones and teach them the ropes. In the beginning of my employment there, I was invited to various compounds and embassies for anything from a party to a musical performance. I was instructed by one of the mentors to attend everything initially and then choose the people I enjoyed being with and the things I wanted to attend, and so I did. I became selective, but even then, I didn't have a free moment other than when I chose to enjoy some space. To this day, I remember the best part of living in Saudi as having the fullest and most fun social life that I have ever been a part of, and I still miss it.

Most of the expats live in a compound behind high walls with military tanks patrolling. There's a boy on each one that looks no more than sixteen, holding a rifle. One hopes that he doesn't start playing with it and fire by mistake. The apartment unit or house is provided by the place of employment, and where we worked, we had units based on our position. As a manager, I had my own one-bedroom unit with marble floors, conference table (what the hell for?), and bidet (wow). The flat was fully equipped with appliances, linens, and dishes. The floors were all marble and the furniture ornate. The compound itself had everything as well—grocery store, jewelry and photography shops, restaurant, swimming pool, and gym. It was entirely possible to never leave the compound other than for the workplace, and that was just across a road. And more rules: No one of the opposite sex was allowed in the apartment after ten in the evening. Really it was no one of the opposite sex ever, but that rule was ignored. Women had separate limited hours in the pool and a black full swimsuit was mandated. I worked for the Saudi government, but on the compounds of large Western companies, the rules were far less rigid or didn't exist at all.

At this point entered Barbara, one of the other nurses who arrived shortly before myself and who had never before traveled outside her own country. It was either a bold or naive move to contract for a year in a country so different from your own and generally hostile toward women. She was from a remote area of Australia where people are very liberal and prone to say whatever they feel at the moment. Basically, if there were rules, when I lived there, I never knew they existed. If they don't like you, they'll tell you straight out. A whole new world of experiences awaited her in the Middle East. She came to work as a nurse in the same department as me, and it didn't take long for the frustrations and challenges to take their toll on her. She was almost in tears many days and deciding whether or not to declare defeat and return home. She took her work most seriously, almost to a fault, and many of the others didn't care or would, it seemed, intentionally put obstacles in her way. It was as though if she did well, they would not look so good.

The team at work was a group of nurses from nine different countries and an equal number of chauffeur-translators, all Saudi males. There was nothing consistent in the standards or education or personality of the others. She worked flawlessly and tried to teach the others the standards but made no friends along the way and therefore had no one to share her frustrations with and no support from the boss. She was the odd one out. Much later, a nurse with the same high standards joined the team, and the two were able to bump their heads against the wall in unison.

I suppose I was initially frustrated myself, but it was a no-win situation. The chauffeurs did everything to get out of work by coming in late, dragging their feet before leaving to take the nurse out to visit the patients and then when with the patients told the patient what they wished rather than what the nurse had requested them to translate. They were extremely cunning as well as charming, and when some of the nurses complained, they would undermine them so it was always the word of the nurse against the word of the chauffeur. I was continuously reminded of the fact that this was a male-dominated country and it was their country I was in. The overall manager was a Saudi female doctor, and she often behaved as though she wanted things in control and offered her support. But once the boys spoke with her, she would back off on any disciplinary action that had been previously discussed. Anyone new who came in to the department was bullied into the existing bad behavior. The most difficult part to understand was the lack of care or concern for the patients under our care.

The Saudi social scene, which we were becoming more and more a part of, and the traveling were what kept us going. The embassies had parties, balls, open bars, and events like concerts more than weekly. There were several private golf courses behind walls, and there were work-sponsored buses for hikes and scenic tours. There were large private companies that had open bars with bands and activities on their compounds. There was somewhere to go every minute you weren't working, and go we did. The weekend was Thursday and Friday, and most weekends, we started on Thursday nights and finished late Friday night in time to get a few hours of sleep before heading for work at seven on Saturday morning. It was a grueling schedule. I suppose for both Barbara and I and most likely for many others, it gave reprieve from the agonies and lack of satisfaction at work. Amazingly, after a few drinks and away from the standards that obsessed her at work, Barbara really loosened up, almost to the opposite extreme. She was as loose as a goose on the dance floor, seemed to keep bringing new people into the group, and had men doing dances around her. Out of the long trousers and lab coat, she let her hair down as in the old movies about nurses and wore bright colors and feathers and outlandish jewelry.

It was so easy to get away from the restrictions; all we had to do was hop on a plane on Wednesday evening and head to Dubai or Bahrain or Oman or Jordan, and you could feel almost like a normal woman—no abaya, sit in coffee shops in the open, go to the latest film in luxury, go to a real nightclub. The funny part was getting on the plane and being the only females not totally covered. Most of the travelers were Saudi and in full regalia when they left Riyadh. When the plane touched down an hour or so later, no one had an abaya on—total transformation. The women were all quite beautiful in their designer clothes and heavy makeup. And even more surprising was to see the Saudi men in the discos, dancing and drinking in their white dresses and red-and-white headscarves. And there were the bars with dancing women that we walked into unknowingly the first time out. There were mostly Russian women, some quite young, standing onstage, swinging to music while the men leered on and then maybe placed money somewhere in the little that was their costume. We didn't stay long in those. In fact, we were asked to leave in one because Barbara attempted to take a photo of the scene.

Then there were the long holiday breaks. We always tried to be gone during Ramadan and Hajj. Ramadan was particular hell. The Muslims fast from sunup to sundown and so all water fountains and soda machines are unplugged. The main cafeteria was closed though they did have a small and separate outside cafeteria where we could eat. A Westerner can't be seen carrying food so we used to hide our little brown bags in our desk drawers and then lock the office door to have lunch. Barbara almost made a fatal mistake the first day into Ramadan and went to heat her lunch in the microwave which was located in the big general office. Not thinking, she paraded back to her private spot with the smell of fish wafting throughout the entire building. She only did that once.

After the first Ramadan, off we went to Egypt, to India, to Ethiopia, to Lebanon; you name it, all those exotic though poor, and sometimes conflict-torn, countries were within our beck and call. We could be out of Fantasyland into other storybook lands. We could do it in style as well because the money was good. We met lots of interesting people, saw all the interesting sights, rode on donkeys at the pyramids, on the back of motorbikes in Jaipur, stinky taxis that were falling apart in Beirut. The list goes on and on.

The first years that I was there, 2003 and 2004, terrorism had become a threat. Several compounds had been blown up, and a number of people killed. The Saudi government very much protected their foreign workers and assured extra tanks, though that didn't necessarily make me feel more secure with the young boys in the seat. There was a Frenchman killed in his driveway, a German assassinated leaving a hypermarket, and an American found beheaded. There were some smaller bombings with destruction of government buildings. The government created a list of the twenty-four most wanted terrorists and set up roadblocks. Within the year, each was caught or killed. It was where I first jumped out of bed and lay flat out on the floor when I heard thunder or any other loud noise. I thought it was a bomb or gunshots. I also learned to deal with my fears through those years.

Fantasyland is not real, and at a point, I felt like I was selling out on my strong value system. I remember sitting at a conference and the woman all had to sit on opposite sides of the room from the men even though they were of the same status professionally. The bright Saudi women were not given credit, often not even listened to. I saw the welts on the back of a young Saudi male from a caning he received for talking to a girl on his cell phone. I saw a beggar in the souks whose hands arms looked like logs, obviously from having them chopped off for stealing. (There was a place called Chop-Chop Square where, until three years earlier, the crimes were punished by chopping off a head or limb. It was a public occasion.) I read the story of a young Malaysian woman who was brought over as a nanny, raped by the head of household, chained to the toilet by his wife to the point of gangrene, and then after losing her hands, had to apologize for causing the problems and sent back to her country as a cripple. I decided if I continued to stay and work there, I was saying that all of that was OK. And so I left.

Barbara stayed. She agreed with what I was saying, and when Westerners gathered, we all voiced our disbelief at the lifestyle. But the money was good, and people all had their various reasons for being there in the first place. The last I heard was that Barbara is still there, though she did change to a different department where there were a few other Westerners working and where she had a support group. She was still partying from Wednesday night to Saturday morning, traveling to yet more exotic places, and sending money back to pay her mortgage on her dream house.

Newsletters from Saudi

19 December 2003
I'm in a Dream or Is It a Nightmare?

Well, here I am, and what a different world this is! The flight from Singapore was fine, and I arrived in Riyadh at almost midnight four days ago, tired, to say the least. I was met in the queue at passport control by the representative from the hospital, and he walked me through the rest of everything and then brought to my new home and left. I have a very large one-bedroom apartment in a four-story building to myself. There are probably fifty apartment buildings on the compound with a small shopping mall in the center. There is also a leisure center and a swimming pool in the compound. I would never really have to leave the compound. The compound is surrounded by army tanks manned by little boys with big guns. Boy, do I feel safe!

Arriving at the apartment was like checking in to a very nice hotel. There was a basket with little goodies like coffee, tea, and biscuits. The floors and entryway table were marble. I have a living room with all the mod cons, a dining room with a conference table, a kitchen with most appliances, even a dishwasher and a bedroom with an attached bath. The bathroom had a bidet with hose: the only thing missing was toilet paper. Now I had been traveling for almost twenty-four hours and was desperate. I searched the place to no avail for any kind of paper. I ended up digging in my suitcase and found coffee filter paper I'd brought and used those. On the evaluation form for the welcome, I did suggest they have toilet tissue as Western staff is not accustomed to hoses or hands for the wipe. The place is air-conditioned and quite comfortable; and at this point, I have no complaints other than the missing toilet paper.

The hospital is about a one-mile walk from the compound, which is part of a much larger compound which houses the hospital, a mosque, an education center, and another very large housing compound with houses rather than apartment buildings. Managers get their own space, hence an apartment. Staff nurses from Europe, North America, and Australia share an apartment with one another. Nurses from South Africa, Malaysia, and a few other countries share an apartment with three others. The Middle Easterners are in a totally different compound with smaller houses, and the Filipinos share with seven others. The pay scale is in much the same order. I'm sure there are many more surprises like that to come.

I attended a hospital wide orientation and still had a few days to go but did walk over to the home health care department to meet the staff I'll be working with. It's a multicultural bunch for sure with staff from ten different countries represented. The uniform for me as a manager is a long white lab coat over a floor-length skirt. I, as a foreigner, do not have to cover my hair. The uniform is fine right now. It's a desert country; and in winter, it gets cold at night and in the early morning, and it's not really hot in the middle of the day. The entire place is air-conditioned. Anyway, everyone seems welcoming, and the Aussie nurse invited me to a Christmas party on the compound so guess I won't have to cry in my milk alone on Christmas.

I have survived the first few days, and there have been no bombings since I arrived. People are a bit tense because it has not been long since the three Western compounds were attacked and the Saudi government has created a list of the twenty-four most-wanted terrorists. I'm sure there'll be much more news to come.

25 December 2003
Merry Christmas from Halfway Around the World

I'm nursing a hangover from that Christmas party last night. Who said Saudi was the place to come if you want to get over alcohol addiction? Even the grocery store on the compound has a complete stock of various grape juices, sugar, and yeast. We brew in the ten-gallon plastic water jugs when they're empty. I met a lot of compatriot doctors and their spouses and others; a very proper Aussie Christmas party it was. There was no shortage of traditional foods or alcohol; they even had Christmas crackers. This is in a country where no other religion is acknowledged or tolerated. The Saudis tend to leave us alone as long as we don't throw it in their face. Discretion is the name of the game. "Merry Christmas" is not something you say aloud to all as you leave the office.

I was given several tips before leaving Australia—one was the recipe for homemade wine and the other, some words of advice. It was to accept all invitations and get on all the social lists when you newly arrive and then pick out the people you want as friends and do the things most interesting to you. I'm finding it good advice because if you say no initially, you may end up in your apartment for all of your days in Saudi. The other bit of advice was to find a limo driver (who is really a taxi driver) whom you trust. They are critical in assuring you get to and from wherever safely and you behave appropriately even when inebriated. From what I've heard about so far, there's a lot going on behind embassy and Western compound doors. I'm trying to make friends as fast as I can and get on all those invitation lists.

10 January 2004
A Very Different New Year

The hospital organizes all kinds of activities for us by bus. They include trips to various sites, the many grand shopping malls, the large supermarkets, and places like IKEA, to restaurants and to the souks (market stalls). It's all here. I've just returned from my first desert trip to the red sand dunes, which are awesome. It chucked down rain the first couple of hours, and I thought I would freeze to death. I spent the first hour in the bus easing the numbness and tingling in the fingers. Once the sun came out, it was an amazing Kodak shoot. My favorite photo was captured with my zoom lens of a group of Saudi males in their white dresses (taubs) and red-and-white gingham headscarves (gutras), playing soccer.

Speaking of which, the males have a total obsession with the headgear. They stand in front of mirrors or a reflecting window and fiddle with rearranging the scarf. I know. I have an office with a reflecting window, and it's been quite the distraction for me. I've noticed at least a hundred different styles. The seemingly more traditional is triangular style like a babushka, but then one tail can be flipped all the way around and over the other shoulder. My favorite is both tails flipped back over the shoulder and rolled into a French twist. I suppose it's the comparison to penis envy in the female; it's the female hairstyle envy. And those dresses, they don't wear much underneath. One can see the contours of the ass. As of yet, I have not been turned on.

I am fully in my job now, and when I'm not writing policies and procedures (at the moment, there is none), I go out into the Saudi homes with the nurses to do supervision. The homes vary from the magnificent to the dumps in the Riyadh shantytown. Indeed, there are poor Saudis—they're the ones not related to the royal family. Shoes always come off at the door. Some houses have a more ornate form of Western-style furniture, but the majority has cushions on the floor so we sit and are often served their cardamom coffee or tea, often with dates or some type of biscuit or sweets. I committed the great faux pas my first time out and accepted a date with my left hand. Being a lefty in Saudi is a major disadvantage. The driver/interpreter very quickly corrected me, and in general, the Saudis have been extremely tolerant of my slow learning of their customs.

The things in the hospital itself that take me by surprise are the customs related to the fundamentalism of the religion. Female doctors are being trained, and the numbers are increasing. They are required to wear the traditional head and face cover so one only sees the eyes. The more fundamentalist ones go as far as wearing black gloves as well, and it's reported that they go from patient to patient to do procedures and never change the gloves. I think that may have to change if their goal is accreditation. Infection control is being compromised. Prayer time is another fascination for me; there is a long corridor which leads along past wards and then finally to the administrative offices. During prayer times, the mats are laid down, and there may be as many as thirty men kneeling and bobbing on the mats. The shoes are in a heap behind them, and the odor of sweaty shoes is overwhelming. I take a deep breath and hold it until I play hopscotch over the back of their legs and reach the other side. And *halas* (that's enough) for today.

End of February 2003
Not Stoned as of Yet

Every day continues to be a new adventure, and at least once daily, I see or learn something that makes me aghast. I have discovered "Chop-Chop Square," so named by the foreign workers. It was not so many years ago that beheadings and limbs were chopped off here for crimes committed. Rumor has it that the announcement was made in the newspaper of the date and the names and crimes. People came to observe as though it was a concert. The foreigners who attended were often pushed right up to the front for the best view and, I suppose, a lesson. It no longer exists as such, my guess due to political pressure. It is now a pleasant square with shops and is near their well-known museum. Beheadings, stoning, chopping off of limbs still does occur, but for us foreigners, not with an announcement. It is a private affair with only the family of both parties in attendance. If we behave badly, we are simply put on the next plane out of Saudi, never to return.

We have the *mutawa* and believe me, the *mutawa* are alive and well and have a hell of a lot of power. They are the religious police and feel very threatened by any loosening up of traditions. They run around in grey woolen *burkas*, heads also wrapped. They may be on the street; they frequent the shopping malls. Generally, they are everywhere there are rules to be broken. They assure that all shops and businesses close during prayer time and chase the men down who are not at prayer. I think their favorite task is chasing foreign women who are not covering their heads through the malls, yelling at the top of their lungs in English, "Cover your head, woman!" In fact, a decree had been made some years earlier that Western women did not have to cover their heads, but the religious police have chosen to uphold the original rule. It is far easier to cover one's head than bear the wrath of the *mutawa*.

I have now been everywhere the buses will take us and there is something scheduled every night of the week. It is mostly about shopping because cinema, concerts, dancing, parties are all forbidden. It is considered sinful but it's funny how the Saudi's frequent Dubai and Bahrain where just about anything goes. Both are only an hour away by plane but, though Muslim, they are a world apart. It's fun to observe on the plane—the women are all in the traditional black abayas and head covers and the men in the *taub* and *gutras* to start. When the plane begins to descend, it all comes off, and it looks more like any other airport in the world.

May, 2004 Tension

I'm sure there's a bit of concern with Saudi being the focus of media attention with the increased terrorist activity at the moment. A German was shot through the head at a distance. He was coming out of a supermarket frequented by Westerners. And then there was the kidnapping of an American contractor. It was followed by his head and body being found months later—separately. And then there's the Frenchman who pulled into his driveway to have someone jump out of a nearby parked car and slice his neck while the wife looked on. Never fear, the Saudis are on to it. We have an increased number of tanks around all the compounds. There are roadblocks everywhere. And we're just not going out at the moment. Just to say I'm safe and only a little nervous.

End of June, 2004
Little Ole Winemaker—Me

I ended on a bit of a tense note in the last newsletter so just to say the Saudis have killed a terrorist on the most wanted list for two days in a row now. That's always more welcome news than that of another Westerner kidnapped and beheaded. I ventured out in the bus to the new Geant French supermarket for the first time in a couple of months. We are beginning to feel somewhat more relaxed. Families of many of the Western and embassy workers have returned to live in their home countries, and some will not return. Activities at the various compounds and embassies are returning to normal, but the roadblocks everywhere remain. I must share one of the poignant moments of the last few months. When the terror escalated, one of the Saudi drivers whom I supervise, but who hates Americans, told me he and his family would take me in and protect me. I was touched. For the longest time, I allowed him to continue to believe I was Canadian as he simply assumed. It is so much easier in the Middle East and actually anywhere in the world to pretend you're Canadian.

Communication is an extremely interesting phenomenon when one lives and works in a foreign country. One learns that even though another may be speaking the same language, they're sure not understanding it the same. English is the official hospital language, but the level of competency ranges from a one word vocabulary of "yes" to perfect fluency without an accent. The result is that things often get said or done, which are not the intention of the person making a request or giving information.

This leads to the why of the newsletter's title. I went to the Tamimi supermarket (better known as Safeway in other countries). My grocery included grape juice, and I requested four boxes, each box being a liter. The bill seemed a bit high, and I simply assumed prices had increased. The delivery was made; I received four cases, or forty liters, rather than four liters. I now have several jugs of wine fermenting in my pantry, and when I return from work and open the front door, it smells like a distillery. The next thing would be to be caught and then try to explain that it's all for my personal use. In fact, I ran around today and bottled it all, and the bottles are hidden under my dirty clothes, behind my smelly shoes and in the very back of cupboards with lots of other things in front.

One cultural perspective this week was the topic of death and how culturally we deal with it. The news has focused on Ronald Reagan's recent death and funeral. It was two weeks of parades and a body being flown here, there, and everywhere. The Muslims, on the other hand, wrap the body in white cloth and toss it into the ground within twenty-four hours. They place a small marker such as a rock on top, wail, and it's finished. There is no fancy coffin or *hoopdela*. When I first arrived, I thought it was insensitive and uncivilized, but after Reagan's funeral, I think of our rituals as even more bizarre. *Maasalaama* (Good-bye).

July, 2004
Towel Boys and Sand

Several of us spent last weekend, the weekend being Thursday and Friday, in Jeddah. Jeddah is another large city in Saudi known to be more liberal as it is near the Saudi Aramco Oil Company, which, for over thirty years, employed foreign professionals. It is also the connecting point for pilgrims traveling to Mecca. I was traveling with friends who were going there for a diving course. We arrived at the Riyadh airport, and lo and behold, there were men everywhere with towels wrapped around them like they'd just come out of a shower or the alternative was something that looked like a white chenille bedspread. It was a Kodak moment I could not partake in. Taking photos in Saudi is another no-no. I learned that the men must show up at Mecca wearing nothing that has seams so they can change anywhere along the way, but they choose to start in Riyadh. As I was going to the beach, I thought that I should probably start in Riyadh in only my bikini, but somehow, that might merit a stoning so the abaya it was.

The Jeddah beaches are not the Mediterranean or Caribbean beaches and are mostly visited for the scuba diving. It was a lazy weekend adding to my suntan. There was another Kodak moment in which a young Middle-Eastern woman walked past in full scuba gear ready to dive, with the black scarf wrapped around her head. I don't think anything ever again will surprise me after Saudi. On another note, we visited the very large modern shopping center here where one can actually get lost. In the food area, men and women were happily sitting together, chatting; the women sometimes without head cover. It almost looked normal, and something totally prohibited in Riyadh. In Riyadh, women are not allowed to sit in any open café or restaurant but behind high screens in rather unpleasant areas without a view.

I remember the time when I was making the decision to come to Saudi to work, being advised of the restrictions and asked how I, as a rebel and free spirit, would cope. At the time, it seemed extremely daunting; but I also love challenges so I took that one on. As I contemplate that now, it certainly is restrictive but not as bad as I anticipated. I think that after thirty years of adapting to various cultures, we generally accept the quirks of the other and become a bit devious in our behavior to get our own needs met. We tend to turn a blind eye to a lot of things. We also laugh a lot at things and events. And we have the balls and concerts and parties behind closed gates at the compounds and embassies. We arrive in our abayas, and once through security, it all comes off, and it's straight to the bar. There are also several golf courses, even some tournaments. One is a nine-hole course at the Intercontinental Hotel. Women are allowed to play, and the only restriction is that we are not allowed to hire a cart because women are not allowed to drive in Saudi.

Early August, 2004
Things Aren't Always What They Seem

It's just another weekend in Saudi, and the temperature is forty-five degrees Celsius, which is about one hundred fifteen degrees Fahrenheit. It's been this hot since the end of May, and when I step out of any building in the daylight hours, it's like stepping into a furnace. During the day, it's a rare thing to see a person walking in the compound; it is unbelievably still. At night, it feels like you've arrived in the Philippines. There are more Filipinos here, I believe, than any other nationality. They were everywhere like ants—on the volleyball court, involved in other competitive sports, in the stands watching and buzzing noisily. In a field area, some were picnicking, and there were children running and playing. For a few moments, I thought I was hallucinating. They obviously have a different tolerance for the temperature than we wimpy white folks do.

The hospital and our units are air-conditioned as well as all the shops. We still walk to work in the early morning for exercise but have resorted to returning home by bus. I've given up golf until the time the weather cools down to tolerable, which I'm told is the end of September. Even the cold water tap sends out almost boiling water. Having a cool shower after coming in from the heat is not possible. Many of the poorer families do not have air-conditioning, and I don't know how they survive. Since it's an extremely dry climate, one has to drink gallons of water. When the urine is brown, it's a sign to top up.

We have had a weird week. We all have satellite TV with both CNN and BBC international news coverage to which I'm addicted. It's my umbilical cord to reality, skewed as that may be. CNN disappeared off the screen and BBC as well for a day. There have been no monsoon rains or sandstorms which might have affected the satellite. There had been a brief news clip about Al Qaeda members who had been killed and a couple arrested, and after that, nothing further. In the Arab News, the main news in English, they broadcast the following day a brief but changed version of the event. Yes, there is censorship. Just when we become complacent because things seem calm and settled, there are little reminders to tell us where we are. I'm reminded when I've said too much in my e-mails because suddenly I have no access for a few days. It's the same with the telephone; there is suddenly so much interference that I must end the conversation. Some of my newsletters have not gone through; I will send this one from the Emirates where I will visit in a couple of weeks.

Another thing which could be an annoyance here, but isn't, is insects. We know there are poisonous scorpions lurking about, mosquitoes, roaches and other weird and wonderful creatures in the insect world, but we never see them. It's because they're blasted from the air with chemicals every other week in the wee hours of the morning. I've never seen such diligence in spraying, and I fear dying from the chemicals and not from a horrid insect. I sleep with my windows open and often forget which day the spraying is done. I wake up choking to the smell.

Mid-August, 2004
It's the CIA Committing the Terrorist Acts!

I have now heard that statement often enough from ordinary Saudis that I think it bears a mention. When the terrorist killings of foreigners occurred earlier in the year, a Saudi I work with whom I have thought of as fairly intelligent told me quite seriously that it was the CIA committing the crimes, and I thought he was kidding. He wasn't, and then several of the others said the same thing in all sincerity. It was their belief. Today at lunch, I was chatting with someone, also Saudi, whom I know, and told him that our department was back out seeing patients in their homes again since things were calmer politically now. He looked me straight in the eye and told me there was no need to worry anyway because it was only the CIA acting, and they had handpicked the ones they were after. What a relief to know that the CIA wasn't coming after me!

He then expounded on his theory. Terrorism was all a CIA plot to harm anyone who would dare to do anything to harm Israel because Israel is actually a state of the United States. In fact, it was the real reason that the US went after Saddam Hussein; he was building nuclear supply facilities to wipe our state of Israel off the face of the Middle East. We had to step in. That sounded extremely far-fetched, even to me, not a huge fan of the American and many other political systems. I listened a bit and then changed the topic; didn't want to destroy his little fantasy.

And with that, I shall give David Letterman something to consider:

TEN WAYS TO KNOW YOU'VE BEEN IN SAUDI TOO LONG

1. Someone gives you some second-hand abayas, and you excitedly run home and try them on thinking, "Oooo, I have a new wardrobe."
2. You look for the hose in the bathroom instead of the toilet paper.
3. Someone hands you a glass of their red wine made from grape juice, and you carry on for an hour telling them what a superb wine it is.
4. An airliner flies overhead, and you hide under the table thinking it's a rocket-propelled grenade or bomber.
5. You have your own driver, cleaner, and hairdresser who come to your house, and you take the limo to work even though it's only a few minutes' walk.
6. A big night out is a trip to the big Safeway supermarket.
7. You're dying for a pork chop even though you've never eaten pork in your entire life.
8. You feel totally naked when you visit another country and don't wear the abaya.
9. Men in white dresses with red and white gingham tablecloths on their heads look perfectly normal.
10. You walk into a hotel room, look for the prayer mat, and ask which way is east.

23 August 2004
Magic Power

I'm so excited. I have been here nine months now and have just figured out what magic power a title holds. I have never been a control freak other than in terms of myself, but I'm learning that in Saudi, if you do not use the power your title gives you, nothing happens. They love titles and degrees here, and the more certificates you carry, the more you can accomplish. It really doesn't matter if you've attended the course; just make sure you get that piece of paper. Already I have a folder one-inch thick with certificates for every little thing I have attended. And I'm expected to hand out certificates for every little informative session I hold for my staff. It is extremely important to have the B.S. and M.S. behind your name. Even our drivers/interpreters have degrees.

For a long time, I wondered why the staff came to me with trivial requests. I would simply explain to them how to go about getting what they needed themselves. They would follow my instructions, and nothing would happen until I became annoyed and sent a forceful memo, using my title of course. Instant magic, the request was answered. A few nights ago, we were on the shopping bus and the driver failed to stop at a designated stop. Another person on the bus politely told him he missed the stop and requested that he go back. He became obstinate and refused telling those who wanted to get off there to take a taxi. I marched up to the front, told him that I was a manager and would be sending a memo with a few copies the following morning. He turned around and returned to the missed stop, though not happily. My secretary orders supplies, and nothing is received. I send a memo with copies to people in high positions, and there is instant gratification.

To top it, I've been asked to speak at a doctor's symposium in December on the need and the future of nursing homes in Saudi. It's only because I know someone in a high position. What do I know about nursing homes? I'm a nurse and home health care manager. I love it, though maybe this magic power thing isn't unique to working in Saudi. It's a good thing that we have an excellent computer system with medical search units and I have a few months to find what I need to know to put together a presentation.

I really enjoy my lunchtime chats with various local staff. I think it's why I bring my own lunch and sit in the outside courtyard to eat in the one-hundred-twenty-degree heat. Today I had an interesting discussion with a young Saudi male, debating arranged marriages as is common in many developing countries versus marriages of love. His argument was that mothers were the ones who chose for their sons though the son is able to voice his request for the qualities he desires; and moms are always right because they are so wise. He then pointed out that in Western cultures, people marry for love and divorce a few years later, marry for another love and divorce a few years later; the cycle repeats itself. How could I respond to that? The Saudis seem to make it last—happily or unhappily.

The other debate that occurs frequently along the same lines is that of having more than one wife for the man. I'm told that according to the Koran, each man is allowed four wives—one for each chamber of the heart. The men feel this is totally justified and that it is a need. Men are not monogamous creatures. It's easy to see—men in Western cultures have affairs and it's often in secrecy and causes anger, pain, and distress. In Saudi, it's simply the rule, and everyone accepts that. Again, I find it difficult to argue against, even though I would not choose to be one of four wives, thank you.

6 September, 2004
Have Returned to Prison

I have just experienced two glorious weeks of freedom in Italy where I met my son for a holiday. We met in Venice rather than in Riyadh where I would have needed papers which take months to obtain to prove that he was indeed my son. In Saudi, a single woman cannot be seen with a man on the street unless he is the husband or son or father. Many of us take that to the limits, and again it seems not to be enforced so much for the Westerners. It's a shame that my son missed the Saudi experience, but then I needed the freedom experience.

Returning was the most difficult part of the holiday, and I really wanted to do a runner, as we say here. It seems to be a common symptom of anyone originating from a free country, the urge to not return to Saudi after a break. It of course means that you've broken your contract and anything you have left in Saudi stays in Saudi. You lose any of the salary and benefits still owing, you pay your own return trip back to your country of origin, and you will never be able to work in Saudi again. I have known a few to do runners; that taste of freedom is strong and makes a lot more sense once one realizes how not normal Saudi is. In the few years I worked there, the sense of doing a runner occurred every single time I had a break from the place, but my sense of responsibility always kicked in.

That is not, of course, to say that I did not become testy. Believe me, I did and often took things to the limit. Alcohol as you know is forbidden in Saudi. On each return, every bag and piece of luggage is sent through very large X-ray machines. On this trip, I bought a beautiful hand-blown Venetian bottle filled with grappa, a rather potent Italian alcoholic beverage. My thinking was that it looked like perfume or liquid soap. I packed it at the bottom of the suitcase and under other bottles. I got caught; the customs officer pointed directly to the place in which the bottle was hidden, opened it, smelled it, and directed me to the office. All the excuses of it being a gift at departure from Italy were ignored. My limo left me, and I ended up spending a humiliating two hours in customs. I paid a big fine and was placed on a computer list of offenders. My brief desire to be returned to the U.S. did not come to fruition. When I asked him to empty the contents and return the empty bottle to me, he refused. So much for trying that one again.

20 September 2004
Don't Miss with Me

Communication is one of my favorite topics. The title above was a bumper sticker on the back of a Saudi car. Even our driver who speaks excellent English was amused. Our interpreters use the expression "Take it or throw it" instead of "Take it or leave it." And yesterday, when I was at the grocery, I bought cheery tomatoes. They're smiling at me, I can't possibly eat them. We had a memo yesterday from administration concerning the working hours during Ramadan, the Muslim fasting period, which will soon be upon us. It made no sense to me, so I asked the Saudi staff. They couldn't understand it either. I ended up telephoning the admin office, and they were in the process of rewriting it because they had so many phone calls. I am currently doing research for the presentation I will give in December. I have read an incredible number of professional articles and research papers in almost unintelligible English. These are the many challenges of working in a non-English-speaking country that chooses to use English as their professional language.

Happy days are here again, and the social scene is in full swing. It appears to be the ball season; there is a formal ball almost every weekend at one of the embassies or Western compounds. They are not cheap to attend, but the proceeds are often donated to the various local charities. I wonder if the charities realize that a lot of the money is from booze profits. I now have a full wardrobe of ball gowns next to all the abayas. We went to the South African embassy a week ago for a celebration and, when leaving, had to check under the car for a bomb. It's the latest little measure in assuring our safety. That was a first for me, and I hope I haven't made it a habit when I return to my home of origin.

We have reached finally the perfect time of year. The mornings and evenings are cool and comfortable and the middle of the day, bearable. I've started wearing clothes under my abaya again. The air-conditioner in the bedroom is turned off and the cold water tap is once again sending out warm rather than boiling water. I can take showers! Humdi l Allah!

8 October 2004
Eid Mubarak

That is the greeting during the four-week Ramadan period of fasting, followed by a week of celebrations. It is significant to the Muslims as is Lent and then Easter to Christians. The definition of fasting is quite different between the two. The fasting I grew up with was no eating or drinking other than water between meals and a small breakfast and lunch, together not more than the dinner. There was only fish, no meat on the Fridays. In Muslim tradition, no food or drink of any kind is taken between sunrise and sunset; after sunset, let the gorging begin. And many eat and celebrate throughout the night. The exception is made for people who are ill, but it must then be made up at some time so many who are ill will choose to fast anyway. The result in hot climates is that the sick become sicker and dehydration reigns. Everyone walks around with no energy, looking like they are on death's door during the daylight hours. An interesting phenomenon occurs in that rice is a large part of the Saudi diet. When the body is dehydrated and the rice reaches the intestines, the intestines pull out all the liquid. There is then an increased number of people coming into the emergency with blocked bowels.

The exact day of the Ramadan is not known in advance and is dependent upon the moon. It is announced at the mosques on the day before it's to begin. And when it does, the impact for us in the hospital is immense. The workday for the Muslims is cut from ten hours to six hours, and we work eight hours basically doing both their jobs and ours. What with the fasting and dehydration and lack of sleep from the night before, they drag around like snails hardly able to move. The biggest muscles moved are the facial ones—to yawn. Far fewer visits to patients in the community are made, but they're suffering as well from sleep deprivation and prefer that we not come out. We are not allowed to show that we are eating or drinking so anything we bring must be in an opaque paper sack. We hide our lunch in the desk drawers because the refrigerator must be empty as well. All the drinking fountains and soft drink machines are unplugged, and some of them are covered. The main cafeteria is shut tight, but there is a small separate cafeteria outside that is kept open for infidels only. Meanwhile, the fasters gain rather than lose weight. Could Allah really have meant it to be this way?

A positive aspect of this season is that they share, the same as we are encouraged to do during the Christmas season. Food baskets and gifts are handed out to the less fortunate ones. We've received very large donations of various items to distribute to our poorer families. As this is only the beginning and there's a long month ahead, there'll be more to report. In the meantime, outside of the work hours, our social life carries on as normal. We just have to plan a bit better in terms of carrying but hiding enough water.

20 October 2004
Beamed in from Another Planet

Most days, we just carry on with our work and personal and social life without thinking a lot about how different life here is from life back home. Outward appearances are normal. The main central avenue of Riyadh is bright, almost gaudy with neon palm trees and lights. The architecture is extremely contemporary, and the road is five lanes wide on each side. I suppose that looking at the odd dress and the Arabic writing on all the shop fronts becomes just second nature after you've lived in the culture for a while. Suddenly, you hear or see something or an incident occurs, and you become very aware of where you are and think you've been taken in a time machine backward from the twenty-first century.

I was reminded of that this week when our youngest of the interpreters, a very normal twenty-one-year-old boy, came to work emotionally very flat and moving like he was in agony. He is normally full of charm and wit and keeps the office alive. I learned after several days from someone he trusted that he had been arrested by the *mutawa* for passing a girl's phone number onto a male friend. He was caned; he received twenty-five lashes across the back. He was barely able to sit but never missed a day of work. Another of our staff, quiet and somewhat timid and always willing to help others out, is sitting in a jail in Yemen, supposedly for crossing into Yemen to collect his brother's children. He was charged to care for the family because the brother was sitting in prison elsewhere. One of our Jordanian nurses had a brother in a Saudi jail for over a year, held without charges. He was released a short time ago and had that broken look.

Filipinos have been arrested for practicing their Christian religions; many articles have been written confirming that. No one is allowed to carry a cross or any other religious item. I went to the souks the other night and was stunned at seeing a man sitting cross-legged in the middle of one of the pedestrian bridges. He had amputated arms and was begging. This was not a normal amputation with stumps remaining. It was as though both arms had been sawed off, like the end of a log. My assumption was that it was the chop for a crime. I don't think he could have attached prosthesis, and I have no idea how he ate, peed, or performed any other activity of daily living. I've read several books now by women who have managed to leave the country after severe abuse, and their stories take me aback. I am living here, complacently going about my life, enjoying parties and an incredible social life while this is going on. My moral and ethical values are being tested; it seems to me that if I continue to work here, I am guilty of ignoring the abuse around me.

On a less serious note, I love interviewing people for positions and reading their applications. A nurse applied several months back, and in answering what qualified her for the job, she wrote in "God-fearing." I interviewed another today. She told me that she would accept it if she did not receive the job because it meant that Allah did not want her to have the job. I spent an hour with her counseling her on the additional experience she would need and how to obtain it. It went in one ear and out the other. Allah would give her the job when he was ready, never mind working to gain the experience necessary for the position. I thought Allah, the good Lord or any other higher being in which we might believe, gives us the tools and it's our job to make use of those tools. The logic here often defies one's imagination.

30 October 2004
Every Day Here Is Halloween

At least it looks that way with everyone running around in what to us is a costume. I attended an embassy Halloween party this past weekend, and guess

---

what the majority who came in costume wore? Abayas and taubs, although with the addition of some extremely ugly masks. We always knew where in the room they were because the boos followed them. At least the bartenders were generous. It's still Ramadan, and we're getting as cranky as those who are fasting. It is not easy to sneak into a closet for even a sip of water.

The biggest news for us at the moment is that our Saudi friend, Osama bin Laden, has resurfaced and made a pronouncement so we wait to see what will happen next, especially with the U.S. elections in a few more days. The atmosphere is somewhat tense. I duck every time I hear a loud noise. I don't know why. It's far more likely that a crowded facility in the U.S. or Europe will be blown up than a building in Saudi. But all motion and talking stop when there's any unusual sound—Pavlov conditioning from living in a country such as this. Politics, kidnapping, and elections are the topics of luncheon conversation. I'm glad the elections will soon be over.

Having a psych background, I put forth my theory. Saudi Arabia is a prime example of a nation with a personality disorder. Individuals are diagnosed with personality disorder, and I've certainly seen it on an organizational level so why not on a national level? A personality disorder is a pathological disturbance of perception, communication, and thinking manifested in cognition, affect, and interpersonal function. Narcissism, paranoia, and manipulation are some of the common traits. The Saudis see themselves on a much higher level than even other Muslim countries; Allah gave them Mecca after all. This carries on into the lack of acceptance of any custom or belief that is not theirs. The paranoia is overtly demonstrated in the way they withhold information, even from one another on a management level within organizations. Often, it's to the detriment of the organization. If I've heard once, I've heard a thousand times the response to a confrontation regarding information or behavior. "Who told you that?" and it is said with venom. Manipulation is the name of the game in the job itself and on a personal level. It is impossible to be direct. If you are, you're the bad guy and all behavior is directed toward undermining whatever it is you're trying to accomplish.

14 January 2005
One Year On

Here's hoping that everyone survived the holidays, whether it be Christmas, Hanukah, Divali, Ramadan, or whatever. I've just returned after my month away and around-the-world flights to visit family during the holidays as well as visit one new country, and this time it was Tokyo. My last night and day before returning to Saudi was spent in Dubai in the Arab Emirates. It's one of Saudi's nearest neighbors and yet a world apart, even though also a Muslim country. Each time I visit, I find it hard to believe the two countries worship the same Allah. It is a place for international meetings and conferences and full of glitz and glamour. It's known for its shopping malls, gold souks, and way-out buildings. I recently saw photos of Dubai thirty years ago, and it was nothing but sand and desert. There are men and women in traditional dresses, but one also sees Middle-Eastern women clad in miniskirts and miniscule tops with tits hanging half out. Men and women can be seen together having coffee at Starbucks or dancing to the music at night. There were still Christmas trees in the malls, and music poured out of every shop. Once again, even a runner to Dubai could be quite acceptable.

When the cat's away, the mice will play, and both I and my supervisor/head of the department were away. Team spirit has never been a strong point of the department, and all efforts at team-building have failed thus far. The manipulation and games are rife and since I've never been much of that kind of game-playing, I have found this, the most challenging and negative aspect of the job, and probably when I quit, it will be exactly for this reason. I feel at times like I'm in a den of snakes. The boys, as I call them (the interpreter/drivers, all Saudi), acted out the entire time I was away, and I returned to extremely frustrated nurses. The boys were signing each other out and leaving work several hours early so were not available to do all the necessary visits. On a few occasions, they would call the patient to say the nurse was unable to visit and then tell the nurse the patient was not at home. The Middle-Eastern nurses coped best because they speak Arabic; the Western nurses were able to cope because they're more aggressive and confrontational; the poor gentle Asian nurses were almost in tears and ready to quit or change departments. The difficulty is that no one will follow through with a disciplinary action because then the boys act out even more. I know that the language barrier is a factor. Help! I will take any advice. I feel like a kindergarten teacher.

Today was the first day of Hajj, the second major Muslim holiday. This is the one-week period the Muslims come from around the world to perform their rituals at Mecca. Last year, a large number were trampled to death in a stampede. All Muslims are mandated by the Koran to perform Hajj once in their lifetime. If a Muslim does the ritual at another time, it is called Umrah and is apparently still acceptable. The staff is entitled to a week off to attend so this is rotated but again another week when absolutely nothing gets accomplished. Of course, they started slacking off last week in anticipation so the one week is actually two. The shopping is in full swing. It is the time when they buy new clothes and renovate their homes. For me, I will just enjoy a week off and stay clear of all shopping malls.

I've made a new best friend who I find delightful and so I must share her with you. I met her in our little networking area where we go to hide for a cigarette break. It's a great place to make contacts—the positive side of smoking. The woman is a Filipina and a secretary for one of the high-up managers. She has a Canadian citizenship and speaks perfect English. She had married a Muslim and converted from Catholicism so must cover her head as a good Muslim does. Her husband insisted they live in Saudi rather than in Canada so that the children would be raised in a true Muslim manner. She keeps us rolling in laughter with her stories. She has taken the children to Bahrain for a pork meal and has even served her husband pork without his knowing (now isn't that passive-aggressive). He did love the chicken. For information, some countries will package pork as veal so that you can bring it into Saudi. The color is much the same. I will share any of her future funnies.

12 February 2005
Mutawa Powa

I believe the *mutawa,* who are the religious police, are the real rulers in Saudi. There are always rumblings on how the royals and the *mutawa* do not always see eye to eye. The royalty gives little hints that they want to move forward into the modern world while the *mutawa* works very hard to maintain the status quo. They have lost some ground but on a painfully slow basis. One of the interpreters said that when he was a child, the *mutawa* would come to everyone's house at the first prayer call to assure that they attended *salat,* the prayers. Each male was obliged to attend beginning at the age of nine or it was jail. Now they seem to focus on keeping women in their proper place and to involve themselves in assuring that change does not take place. I heard one tale of a foreign pregnant woman falling down an escalator due the *mutawa* coming up behind her and whipping her with a cane because her head was uncovered. It was not that long ago, but due to the incident it created, they are prohibited now from any form of caning in a mall; instead, they scream at the individual loudly enough that everyone in the same vicinity of a mall can hear and say, "Shame on you."

Saudi had their first election ever yesterday. Women were of course not allowed to vote and certainly not to run for any position. But hey, voting itself was a big step. The campaign was an amusing process and clearly not anything like the campaigning leading to an American election where one starts praying six months before that it will be over soon. I don't turn on the news for the year before, and it's the lovely thing about working overseas—I don't have to suffer the agony of that. The campaign here didn't hog all the networks. Here, it lasted only a week or two. There were marquees set up all along the main roads where the men could stop to ask questions and get information about the candidates. There was no hoopla leading to the election; in fact, I only learned about it from my brother in the U.S. There were no incidents during the election and not a lot of complaining or challenging afterward. I'm sure that they were all minor positions and not that of a presidency.

And for my favorite topic—here is the latest on the work scene. I am in a total stand-off with the chief of my department, and I could be out of here sooner rather than later. Each nurse has a desktop computer as all patient documentation is done that way. The office is an open office without personal lockable space, and each nurse has a cubicle. We were each presented with a form which included a statement that we would take full responsibility for our assigned computer. That means that if any damage is done to it or it is stolen, we pay for it. I refused to sign and explained to the nurses the responsibility they were accepting if they chose to sign the document and stated I would support them if they didn't. People wander throughout the office the entire day. The interpreters sit and download their rubbish, often porn, at the nurses' computers. Where is the logic in an individual having to take responsibility for an expensive piece of office equipment for which they have no control over?

The social scene is really the reason I remain in Saudi. It only gets better and better the longer I'm here. The ball season is upon us once again, and I seem to spend half my life in Saudi in one or another embassy. We tend to give each a rating. The British Embassy provides the best food (hard to believe that with their culinary history but obviously they have hired the best chefs). The ambassador shows himself and does a walk-through in an event. The American Embassy has the most going on but the most expensive booze. Uncle Sam's has bacon burgers to die for, making the cost of booze worth it. The ambassador never shows his face; he is obviously the most paranoid, and I suppose that's not news to anyone. The Canadian Embassy has wonderful classical concerts, but sorry, only tea and coffee are served. The German Embassy is our favorite. They have the occasional visiting pastor and a regular five-star happy hour. They never measure the pour and are extremely generous. The bar and dance area is in a Moroccan theme so there are the cushions and the hubbly-bubbly to smoke. The ambassador and his wife are charming and are always part of the gang. One especially good night, they walked us to the gate, their little dog in tow, and waited until we were safely in our limo.

20 March 2005
It May Be Palm Sunday, But It's Just Another Day in Saudi

There are no palms or long sermons here, and the Christian holy week will go by quietly until Friday when I sneak to an Easter service, as to where, I choose not to print. CNN television did cover news on how Palm Sunday was celebrated in various parts of the world, and it was not blocked. Of course, it could suddenly just go off the air for a few days; it's what normally happens when a channel misbehaves. Anyway, there are no colored eggs, chocolate rabbits, or Easter bonnets again this year, only me in my black abaya and headscarf, drinking my home-brewed wine.

I've just returned from Lebanon, but that is another story. It is again a Muslim country where difference is tolerated and again makes it extremely difficult to return here. The façade here is incredible and, to the outside world, looks very good indeed. The Western foreign employees lead the good life, earn a substantial salary, and have our indiscretions generally overlooked. We are to be the communicators for Saudi and tell the world what a grand place that it is and what wonderful, intelligent, and high-tech people inhabit it. The Western governments hide their dirty laundry so the oil keeps flowing. And believe me, the dirty laundry pile is gigantic. The majority of Saudis live without any basic freedoms or human rights, and the workers from other poor nations are under the threat of abuse. Young women are hired from the Philippines, Malaysia, and Bangladesh as domestic help for rich Saudi families, only to become slaves. This is not true in all cases but often enough for us to be aware of it. The pay is low, and they support entire families in their countries of origin so they have no choice. I certainly do and am thinking more and more that this is not OK.

2 April 2005
Tsunami?

A couple of weeks ago, we arrived at the office after the weekend and found our entire office floor covered with two inches of water. The water does drip in through the ceiling when there's heavy rain, but the weekend had been hot and dry. Every staff member turned detective and searched in all the nooks and crannies for a culprit and made diagnoses, though an overt cause was not found. The maintenance people arrived an hour later, only to do exactly the same exercise, again with no results. I missed yet another Kodak moment as all our Saudi interpreters hoisted their dresses, giving the appearance of tiptoeing through the tulips. Some had big bloomers under their dresses, and others, nothing but hairy legs. I was thankful no one hoisted up far enough to notice if they were wearing a G-string or nothing at all. The women did all the work, getting things up out of the water while the boys stood by and looked on, still of course giving opinions as to what might have occurred. To date, the problem has not been found and, like many other problems, probably never will. I'm simply blaming it on a tsunami that never made it as far as our housing compound.

There are more and more Middle Easterners, therefore Muslims, moving into the housing compounds. The more that come, the more restrictions there will be. I have one living above me. I hear the thump-thump of high heels constantly on the marble floors. She has had the Arab music on full blast as she dances around, driving me mad. After having to listen for a few hours the other night, I turned on my washer, which has a very loud two-hour cycle at one thirty in the morning before retiring. Tit for tat.

On a positive note, I have mentioned how important certificates and diplomas are. Hence, so is ongoing education. We have a wonderful library, medical search units on the computer system, and frequent symposia and workshops. Many of the symposia for nurses and doctors are held at the posh Riyadh hotels and have a conference fee of approximately $30, which includes not only the education but gargantuan buffets. The males sit on one side of the auditorium and the females on the other. There is no mixing here either. The hospital provides transportation to and from, and we're always given a briefcase or file folder. You can also stash up on notepads, pens, chocolates, and occasional duffel bags and medications. I go as often as I can. The annoying part is that people will chat away right through the presentations. They keep the cell phones turned on and don't bother lowering their voices. It's extremely disruptive when you are there for education. It's like the New York Stock Exchange at the start of a business day.

I'm already planning my holiday for the autumn. That's one way we cope—by thinking from holiday to holiday. It will be the Botswana and South Africa this time during Ramadan. I refuse to be in Saudi for the next one.

18 April 2005
It's a Four-Embassy Weekend

So you think we're suffering in a country where we can't go out without an abaya, where we can't talk to a man unless we're married or closely related to him, where as women, we can't sit on the outside at a Starbucks, where we can't drive even golf carts, and where booze, church, and any symbolism of Christianity, pork, dancing, and cinemas are illegal. Let me tell you all the ways we suffer. Here's my schedule for the next week:

21—British Embassy Benefit—real stuff to drink and a harem of men to dance with

23—American Embassy—happy hour with the real stuff, men, and bacon burgers

25—Aussie Embassy—Anzac day service and breakfast, Bundy's rum at seven in the morning

26—German Embassy—Archeological film followed by reception with the real stuff

27—Leg of lamb barbecue at another Western compound

28—Costume party with dancing, buffet, and the homemade stuff at another compound

29—American Embassy—Pig and champagne celebration

I'll never have this indulgent a lifestyle again. That is a fairly typical week when things are politically calm and the terrorists are in check. Learning to say "no" and getting more than four hours of sleep in a night are by far the hardest thing we have to do—at least when we're not at work.

I want to describe one of the real joys of working where the group is multicultural and where I believe the real reason lies for staying in a country such as this. It's the people and friends from everywhere and the realization that we really are all more alike than different. We hold each other up when we need to; we make sure we're on each other's list for whatever is happening; we don't judge but rather share stories and unbelievable moments; we laugh with and at each other a lot; we respect each other by not crossing the line and getting in each other's pants. Meet my circle of friends. There's Lauren, a Lebanese, fifty-five-ish, flirt of all flirts, and when you give it back, runs like a scared rabbit. He's been here over twenty years. Another man who's been here a very long time is Michael, a very Irish Yank who looks after all of us like an old woman. His wife is in the States but he is a good boy, unlike so many others who leave families behind. Raja is one of the younger members of the group, Indian-English, the perfect boy and gentleman, always buying everyone a drink, and he's an excellent golfer. There's Larry, Aussie/Kiwi, a bachelor who would love not to be. He's waiting for one who knows he's waiting for her. He's our perfect male companion, easygoing and loves everything. There's our married couple, Rolf and Tina. He's German, and she's South African. They've been here the longest, and sometimes I wonder if they'll ever leave. He's a master brewer, and she has the heart of gold. Last but not least is Brittany, an Aussie from Tasmania, a teeny-tiny woman, quiet and reserved one might think, but put her on the dance floor, and off she goes.

Others come and go, but that's the inner circle. I must mention also Mahmud, our consistent limo driver. He's Egyptian with a family back in Egypt. He adores his family and brings them to Saudi when he can. Otherwise, he is our protector. He takes us everywhere and will drop any other request if we call. If any of us has had too much to drink and is acting stupid, he becomes quite firm to assure we behave appropriately for the Saudi standards until we're back into our own apartment. He's very Muslim but turns a blind eye to our indiscretions. He's definitely a keeper. Someone who really needs an honorable mention is Mohammed, our office cleaner from Bangladesh. When I arrived, he did not speak a word of English but was desperate to communicate. A lot of gesturing and sign language went on. In a year, he is speaking and understanding very well. He was a doctor in his own country but was able to earn more to support his family by coming to Saudi to work as a cleaner. Recently, he was cleaning the floor with the electrical machine, obviously not maintained properly, and was electrocuted as we all stood and watched. Someone did have the sense to pull the plug and wheel him to our emergency room. He was none the worse for wear.

1 June 2005
Who Says This Isn't a Developing Country?

How one perceives oneself is often quite different than how others perceive them, and sometimes, one can be offended by that difference. Most Saudis are horribly offended when they see or hear anything that indicates that they are a developing country. They see themselves as a Utopia, a place where everything is perfect and everyone should be content. Heaven forbid that they hear any information to force them to think critically about themselves, particularly in the areas of politics, human rights, and religion. But then I suppose this is not a fault of Saudi alone. The U.S. is prone to its own egotism and not being open to criticism.

My little commentary stemmed from a silly little article in *The Arab News: Home Mail Delivery to Start in Riyadh*. Here is a country with the most modern of architecture, all the newest of technology, and mail delivery is a new thing. A few blocks from the big shopping malls are dusty dirt roads leading to areas where Bedouins are living in tents with no electricity and no mailboxes.

My biggest area of concern is the inequity of treatment within the foreign workforce. The Westerners are treated on an equal par though they usually take the credit for any innovations, but the others are treated as slaves. We get flash housing; they get substandard temporary units. We travel in air-conditioned buses, they're packed like cattle in the back of trucks and vans. We get our midyear and our annual leave; they're lucky to get leave every other year. I couldn't live a day on what they make in a month. How is that fair? It isn't in my definition of "developed."

The hospital of course shines. Our hospital is one of the hospitals well known for separating Siamese twins, and very challenging separations they are. The twins often are brought from the poorest of countries where surgery is not possible and where the family would be unable to pay for such a procedure. It seems to me though it is not done as a philanthropic gesture but rather as a "see me and how well I take care of others," almost sleazy gesture. The upcoming event is posted on huge billboards in many locations, and the surgery itself is televised. The hospital has eight hundred beds, all on one level. Amazing. We have no lack of exercise capability. It's possible to get knocked down by a golf cart. That is how big the place is. The dietary, laundry, and supply carts are trains pulled by a motorized vehicle. And on the roads outside the hospital, families drive with a mob of kids in their vehicles, not strapped in. If it's Allah's will for an accident to occur, it will anyway. Women are unable to sign for any of their own procedures; it has to be the husband or the nearest male relative. Once again, is this a developed country? And that is today's sermon, all because they're installing a mail delivery system in Riyadh.

Tying into this, I've just attended another symposium, and it was the best that I've been to. It was titled *"Globalization and Adolescence."* It was amazing to hear so much said behind the conference doors. There are definitely two camps with very different belief systems here. The hard-core fundamentalist that everything is as it should according to the Koran, and therefore there is a denial that teenagers have sex before marriage and that children are sometimes sexually abused. It's against the religion, and no Saudi Muslim would participate in such an act. The other camp is more reality-oriented and is saying it's time to open the eyes and admit that things do happen—the same kinds of things that happen in the rest of the world. One doctor was extremely upset in reporting that a thirteen-year-old pregnant girl was turned away from the hospital because the hospital did not want to be involved in the publicity of having to notify the police. She aborted outside the hospital doors. A very healthy discussion ensued. I was relieved to know that even though things aren't said aloud, there are people who are aware and thinking. There is some hope for change.

25 June 2005
Progress

I've just returned from a wonderful two weeks in Tunisia, my favorite Muslim country located in North Africa. I did not try to bring in any Tunisian wine this time. The reentry process was smoother, but the will to return wasn't. I've started the countdown to the next holiday.

I had responses from many of you asking me how I can live here as negatively as I present things in my communications. My response to that is that I present things as I see and feel them. There are negatives and positives in every culture. I assure you that this not a negative experience, and I have no regrets at my choice to come and work here. Things that are different for an individual get noticed then talked and moaned about. I think we're creatures of habit, and we don't like to be uncomfortable. Differences initially make us uncomfortable. My time away always allows me to look on and contemplate the whys and the personality dynamics of the culture at play. I've been here long enough now to have many acquaintances, and almost all agree that we would not trade this experience. There's black and white in everyone, everywhere, and everything. Some of the things that I perceive as negatives were common practices in our own country not so long ago. These people came out of the desert as nomads around thirty or forty years ago, thanks to the world's dependence on oil. I guess when you have a commodity that everyone wants, you'd become cocky as well. The changes in this country in thirty years outweigh the progress we've made in that same amount of time.

12 July 2005
Fundamentalism Played Out

I'm back on this topic because of the recent terrorist attack in London and that impacted me more than 9-11 only because we lived five years there and never in New York. My kids grew up in London so it's near and dear to my heart. And for me, the key word here is "fundamentalism" and not "Muslim." Al Qaeda is a terrorist organization which does not have the support of the Saudis any more than it does of any sane government. When an attack happens, though, it brings religion and the irritants of that to the forefront. I'll share some of the behaviors that to me are both annoying and amusing at the same time.

Prayer time or *salat* is five times per day, and though the women in this country are not allowed in the mosques, they still must pray, and so they find anywhere they can. In airports and public buildings, it's often the restrooms or toilet areas which I personally would find off-putting. In our facility, they use the toilet area only for the cleansing and then lock up our conference room for their prayers, putting all other business on hold. The female toilets are always covered with water everywhere. I was always sitting down to a wet toilet seat, so I no longer sit because I don't know if it's water from the cleansing or urine. Neither is anything I want to sit upon. I feel for the Bangladeshi cleaner, but then he probably understands it better than I do.

All shops including those in malls are closed during prayer time. This is only in the fundamentalist countries. The bus often drops us at the mall, prayer time begins, and we have to go back out and wait until prayers finish before we can continue our shopping. We did have one favorite hypermarket. Instead of chasing us out when *salat* begins, they locked us in. We shopped in peace and checked out when everyone else returned from prayer. Alas, good things never last. The *mutawa* caught on and threatened the store managers.

I work with a lovely Saudi woman who had grown up in the States secondary to her father's job. She did her schooling and university there. She returned to a managerial position in the hospital—a well-deserved one. She did not cover her head or face. My boss didn't either for a long time. The *mutawa* supposedly have no jurisdiction within the hospital grounds, but apparently, the Saudi women are hassled. I returned after my holiday to find her covered. Her demeanor has changed along with the cover. I learned from the Middle Eastern staff that the Saudi women are sent threatening letters until they conform. And they all do.

In the same vein, I learned that at the moment, Saudi and Bahrain are in a standoff with each other. As I have mentioned several times, Saudi women by law are not allowed to drive any vehicle; they are even forbidden bicycles after the age of puberty for fear the hymen will break. Women going to school in Bahrain often obtain a driver's license while there. Many women drive when they are visiting in the country. The *mutawa* has caught onto that and are raising the issue and demanding that Bahrain stop allowing the women to drive. The debate goes on, but only the males are given a voice. As the Saudis get more exposure to the rest of the world's practices, the *mutawa* tighten their rein. Many men are in favor of women driving. The men must leave their job to take the wife and children to school or to the doctor. There's a lot of missed work time secondary to this law.

25 July 2005
Liver and Delivery

I found a message from my secretary: "Return telephone call to Liver and Delivery." I asked her if she meant the liver unit or the labor and delivery unit. She responded by telling me that it was definitely the liver and delivery so I telephoned my friend who worked in the liver unit to see if the unit had been renamed. I still roll on the floor with laughter at some of the misuses of the language. The day only continued to go downhill from there. The interpreters informed me that the recent terrorist bombing in Egypt's Sharm el Sheik resort area was caused by Bush and not terrorists. What can you say but "Oh really!"

I've learned another bit of Moslem trivia. It seems that there are as many mosques in Moslem countries as there are pubs in London and Dublin. The reasoning is that each time one builds a mosque, they are assured a place with Allah. I know the pubs are a lot more fun. I spoke with my ten-year-old granddaughter yesterday and she asked me why women had to cover their heads and faces with veils. How does one answer that? I told her it was because women are ugly, we're a terrible temptation, and because men just can't help themselves if we don't. We laughed, but I really can't answer that one. I'm in awe at the number of women who do convert because it's beyond my comprehension that anyone would convert to a religion in which they have no freedoms or rights. Women here aren't even allowed to authorize their own health care.

30 August 2005
Miracles, *Gahwah*, and Crouching Dragons

We had our own little miracle in the department the same day the Air France plane crashed in Toronto and all the passengers walked off alive. Our Bangladeshi cleaner, pushing along a floor buffer twice his size, was electrocuted before our eyes. It was due to frayed wire on the equipment. He was glued with his hands to the handles, and his body was convulsing. I was in my office in a meeting when I heard the flurry of activity outside my door. Our Aussie nurse was a quick thinker and stepped in to take charge. She gave instructions to pull the plug from the outlet and others had him in a wheelchair in seconds and on his way to the emergency room before I knew that anything had occurred. He was breathing when disconnected from the electricity. When doing the incident report, I discovered that it was known the wire was frayed because it was wrapped with clear cellophane tape rather than electrical tape. Dah.

Gahwah is the nourishment of life in this country, and I doubt anyone would survive without it. It is coffee brewed with cardamom, a strong anise-like spice. As a coffee drinker, I cannot call it or substitute it for my coffee because it doesn't have that strong coffee bean flavor. Oh, the Saudis love our kind of coffee as well. It's rare to see a Saudi walking down the corridor without a cup of coffee in hand. I suppose with alcohol banned as a social stimulant, coffee is a replacement. Since I arrived two years ago, three coffee shops—Starbucks-style—have opened within the hospital walls. There are the lattés and espressos and all the racks of coffee paraphernalia for sale. Each has the café tables and chairs where staff sit and discuss all manner of things while the aroma of coffee wafts through the hallways. It is a far nicer smell than urine.

Today, I was walking along the corridors on my return from collecting referrals on the wards and suddenly a sight I see every day here in the hospital just tickled my funny bone. The Saudi men in their white dresses and checkered scarves sat everywhere in crouching position on the floor in the out-patient department waiting for their appointments. There were plenty of empty chairs about, but crouching is the preferred position. I couldn't help but think of the movie title "Crouching Dragons." Their pelvic floor muscles must be like elastic steel. It may well be worth doing a research study to find if they have less incontinence in old age in comparison to their Western counterparts.

Earlier in the weeks, I again went on home visits with the nursing staff. One visit was to a tiny old woman with contractures following a stroke; she was left in the care of a young Filipino nurse while the family worked. The nurse spoke good English so the interpreter stayed outside. I noticed that there were two beds in the room, one for the patient and the other for the caregiver. There was no TV or other extras. I asked a few questions and learned more than I think I wanted to learn. The nurse had a two-year contract—no days off and 24 hours per day. Her pay was $100 a month. There was no entertainment source and no one to talk to as the patient was fully demented. It seemed more like a prison sentence than a job. She started crying as she related her circumstances and said that she was afraid to ask for anything because her sponsors were good people. She begged us not to tell anyone what she had shared with us. I've heard that kind of story more than once. I sent over some books and puzzles in hopes it would ease her boredom a bit.

I've had another week away; I know you are all wondering when I do work. I visited Cypress and then the south of France, where my granddaughters joined us. I returned with lice and now I am learning from our Chinese-Malaysian nurse traditional methods of getting rid of them. She has me washing my hair with compote of pureed lemons and limes, and it is slimy. Each day when I arrive at work, she picks out the eggs. I think it is working and highlighting the hair at the same time.

16 September 2003
This Just Ain't Normal

I've just met with a pleasant young Egyptian sales representative from a medical products company. He's another doctor who makes more money selling in Saudi than practicing as a doctor in his own country. We did discuss his products but then went on to social chit chat. He's Muslim but as frustrated with Saudi as am I. We agreed that it is just not normal and it's absolutely necessary to get out every few months to survive. People come from many nations, often to get money to feed their families, get rid of debts or a husband or a wife, build a home—in their own country, and other things which they could not normally afford. And the Saudis pacify us. They give us just enough to keep us beholden. Almost everyone returns somewhere else when they achieve their goals. No one opts to stay in Saudi as they might in Europe or Australia other than the poor wretches who have chosen to marry a Saudi and have given up their option to choose.

It's been interesting to see how people from various other cultures cope. Each has their own way of viewing a job and job expectations and then reacting and performing. The Malaysians in general are extremely nonconfrontational and bear their pain in silence. As a Yank, I've had to learn how to zip it up at times, and that's not easy for us. I may think I'm right for example about a nursing standard and the Middle Eastern nurse feels it's more important to keep the patient happy. This may be the first time I've really had to examine my own values in depth and sometimes let go, even if I don't agree. After all, who is to say which is correct in terms of values?

The sense of community is another thing that seems to result when there is a cultural mix in a totally foreign environment. Each cultural group has very strong ties and socializes more with each other than with other different cultures to the point of being a clique. On the other hand, each person is caring and is there in times of need. An example happened this last week. I got off the shopping bus after a trip to the supermarket, toting enough groceries to last a year. I was struggling with all the bags when a South African woman came from behind and scooped up half the bags without saying a word and walked with me all the way to my door. I didn't know her until then.

16 October 2005
And the Light Bulb Came On

Culture shock is not a new phenomenon to me, but by now, I thought I was totally immune. I remember moving to Tunisia thirty years ago expecting culture shock but experienced awe instead. I moved to England twenty years ago not expecting culture shock and I did get it—big time. I was going to another English-speaking country, but in fact, not even the language was intelligible at times. I think the culture shock was greater because I didn't expect it at all. Then there was Australia, and the only culture shock that really impacted me was the Australian directness; we can't hold a candle to them in terms of saying it the way it is. I came to Saudi knowing full well that it was going to be one really weird place and was fully prepared. Up until recently, I thought I'd done quite well. But after the last month of no sleep because of the work culture and nausea at the mere thought of having to go into that office, the light bulb came on. I am suffering from severe—although I hope reversible—culture shock.

I've continuously said that I love being in a multicultural setting where we work together to achieve a common goal. We have potluck lunches to honor each one's birthday or someone leaving and taste and love everyone else's traditional dishes. There may be a melding of the foods but, I'm beginning to believe, not of the minds. The intellect is the same, but the process of implementation is not. The goals are not also really the same, and I have to look at it on Maslow's hierarchy of needs. We have all arrived but not at the same stage of where we are in terms of having had all our emotional needs met.

Maslow's hierarchy of needs was introduced in 1943 by Abraham Maslow and is explained by Kendra Cherry on About.com guide. It is a pyramid demonstrating how people are motivated to fulfill basic needs for food, water, and sleep before moving on to high levels. The next level is for safety and security, and when that is achieved, love and intimacy. The last level is self-actualization and is that ability to also be aware of other's needs and help them achieve those without personal gain.

I try to look at selfish behavior, particularly in the workplace, in those terms. Many of the Middle Easterners have experienced conflict in their own countries since birth and may have had food and water, but never safety and security. A few have come from Palestinian refugee camps in Jordan and may even have struggled for food and water. They've had to learn manipulative behavior and often aggression at a very young age to get even their most basic needs met. And then there are the poor women in Saudi, often highly intelligent and educated without even the right to make a decision about their own health care or the choice to leave an abusive marital relationship. Having a theory base helps me a great deal to understand the often destructive behavior, both to self and to the workplace, but it doesn't make it any easier to deal with.

At the moment, it's escalating into another Iraqi conflict zone in our office. Everyone is hearing and interpreting everything totally differently. The interpreters are simply leaving early and then lying the next day about their whereabouts. When they did make visits with the nurses, they rushed them through, and they have the power to do that because they are the only one actually able to communicate with the patient and family and they have the vehicle. When I report the behavior to my boss—a Saudi female—she is bullied by the interpreters because she is a female and has no power in a male-female meet. Me thinks this is a losing battle, and it is time to move on. I have given them the tools and the education to achieve their goal of accreditation. The rest is up to them.

12 December 2005
Christmas in Saudi—Not!

Well, I survived another Ramadan by leaving the country of course; this time, it was almost a month in Africa on safari in Botswana then an elegant historical train from Victoria Falls in Zimbabwe to Cape Town in South Africa. On my return, I finally did it. I've turned in my resignation. At the moment, my emotions are mixed. After two years, I have met so many special people and have made a lot of dear friends. I will hate returning to a boring social life and not having money to burn. I will miss the ease of traveling to so many different countries so nearby, but I don't want to stay long enough to become embittered.

It's Christmas season, but there's no way to really tell other than behind walls and doors. There are no Santas or decorated trees on the outside, and I can't decorate my office door. I had a screen saver on my computer with pine trees covered in snow, and someone changed it while I was away. I guess it looked suggestive of the Christmas holiday season. It's another story behind closed doors. The embassy parties are in full swing with abundant holiday décor. There's an outdoor bazaar on almost every compound, selling Christmas wares and crafts. People have been extremely creative in what they've put up as trees and decorated with homemade ribbon and ornaments. Even the Tamimi supermarkets are selling turkeys, cranberries, and canned pumpkin.

I have scheduled the few Christians who work with me for as many days off as possible during the holiday period. A few of us are going to Oman for the holiday. Though another Muslim country, they are tolerant of differences, and I've learned they decorate for the foreigners and all the hotels have Christmas parties and dinners. So merry Christmas to all and a happy New Year!

19 January 2006
My Bucket Floweth Over

I'm hoping everyone enjoyed the holidays. Oman was a lovely country; the people are soft-spoken and but friendly, traditional in abayas, *taubs,* and *gutras,* but tolerant of other dresses. The country is a pristine blend of ancient and modern. The most touching event for me was a Catholic mass held on large park ground next to the church. It is normally frequented by Filipinos. There were over a thousand people in attendance under the starlight, and the priest walked through the crowds passing out the communion. This was in a predominantly Moslem country.

Now the countdown of sleepovers begins. When I was new, someone said to me that I must think of the experience as filling two buckets—one you fill with the money you make, the other you fill with the shit that you deal with. You leave Saudi when either one of those buckets is filled. Knowing my penchant for spending, you know which bucket flowed over.

Most recently, I've still had second thoughts of leaving so I did a stay-leave list. Here it is:

Stay	Leave
Money is tax-free.	Getting it is a struggle; they screw us at times.
Travel	Getting through Riyadh's airport
Sunshine every day	And one hundred twenty degrees, six months of the year
Grand shopping malls	Can't jump in a car and go
Golf, desert hikes, bowling	No skiing, bicycling, treks in the woods
Lots of balls and parties	It costs a bomb.
Free nice accommodation	They're starting to move in the Saudis.

Fashion is cheaper.	Must cover them with an abaya
More booze than imaginable	Save the liver and brain cells.
Multicultural work setting	Westerners do all the work.
Lots of men	The majority wear dresses.
Excellent cafés and restaurants	No wine; we eat behind a screen.
The list could go on.	

9 February 2006
Times, They Are A-changing

I've been here two years and two months now, and this will likely be the last newsletter from Saudi. Believe it or not, in such a fundamentalist place, change does occur. The pace of change often catches me off guard. I've mentioned the photos I saw of Riyadh thirty years ago; it was a desert, and now it's a city of eight million and growing rapidly. The population is expected to triple by 2024. They of course did have help with the discovery of oil; and now, the televisions bring them the news from around the world. I love watching the interpreters at work strutting around in their traditional garb with cell phones and iPods stuck in their ears, and whenever we're not using the computers, they are.

Years before I came, some close friends worked for several years in Dammam near Jeddah. They spoke of the stoning and the chopping of limbs. That is no longer visible. I went to Kingdom Tower, one of the well-known malls this past week, and my mouth went agape. I hadn't been there in a year. There were young boys dressed in baggy jeans hanging low and baseball hats turned backward, roller-blading. Young women had their veils slung back, makeup to the hilt, and texting on their cell phones. There was no *mutawa* in sight. There came even a bigger surprise when I waited in front of the mall for the bus. Several young men went flying by on Harleys, rearing up on the back wheel. This would not have happened a year ago. Who knows what changes will come in ten years' time? Women might be driving. Heaven forbid!

ETHIOPIAN ESCAPE

I was working in Riyadh in the mid-2000s, and any place to visit on a weekend or for a few weeks was an escape, not the normal kind escape that most folks take, but an escape it was for me to Ethiopia. I suppose this is because I love visiting places that most tourists dare not go. And actually, I was escaping from another Hajj when Muslim men dressed in white towels and women in white nun costumes come from everywhere in the world to do their once-in-a-lifetime mandatory pilgrimage to Mecca. We were lucky in the fact that Saudi was central to some fairly unique as well as some troublesome countries and air flights were short and sweet and cheap.

Ethiopia had been a place of interest for me since the seventies, when as a family, we had lived in Tunisia, a small country in North Africa. Project Hope, a medical aid organization, had arrived in Tunisia from Ethiopia. The story that I remember was that they had a mission there and had evacuated because several medical workers from another organization had been kidnapped and safety had become an issue. There was a lot of tension at that time. I also remembered photos in the media of starving children with big bellies and appeals for money. There were years of conflict, and even presently, the country is unstable and the people are extremely poor with many still starving.

Ethiopia was called Abyssinia in the very early days and dates back a thousand years. It has been independent, the only African country not colonized. It has roots tracing back to ancient times, before the birth of Christ. It has its own time system, seven years behind Gregorian time, which is what the rest of the world uses. It also has its own alphabet. The Axumites were the original people, and the Solomon dynasty, which claimed descent from King Solomon and the Queen of Sheba, existed until the death of Halie Selassie in 1975 while under house arrest. A skeleton was found dating back 3.2 million years and was thought to be a missing link between ape and man. Lucy, as she is called, rests in the archeological museum in Axum. Christianity was adopted as the country's religion in A.D. 400 though many are Muslim and there are still some Jewish colonies.

It is unique in its religious history, and the disputed belief, the Ark of the Covenant (ten commandments), had made its way there centuries ago through Egypt and was located in Axum in the north. The religion of the country is mainly Coptic Catholic and has not changed since the beginning. Due to the differences in the calendar, there are variances in when the religious holidays are celebrated. We had just celebrated our Christmas in Oman where other religions are allowed their practices and arrived a few weeks later to the Coptic Christmas celebrations in Addis Ababa. My shock was to see a tall skinny ebony Santa walking down a main street, ringing a bell. Later, we were invited by a group of young university students to a Christmas party they were having, and of course, we went.

Addis isn't a bad city as African capitols go. The streets are paved. There are shops and small shopping centers; there is the normal huge central market with stalls carrying everything from coffee, fruits and vegetables, to crafts and clothing. The central markets are always extremely crowded, with beggars hanging around the outside, little kids running around begging to carry your sacks for a tip, and pickpockets. Not surprisingly, there were some shocking sights on the streets. An example was of a man with totally deformed legs, moving himself on a low to the ground wooden cart with small wheels, using his hands to propel. There was the makeshift housing on the sidewalks along a main thoroughfare either made of torn canvas or corrugated tin laid on some supporting sticks. No matter how often I've seen this sort of thing, even now, it still unsettles me that human beings are forced or choose to live this way.

The scammers are without a doubt present, and though I'm always vigilant, scammed we were. The students who invited us to their party were absolutely charming. They were dressed well, spoke very intelligently, were fluent in English, and led us into very interesting discussions. They danced for us in their traditional dress. We were thrilled to be invited for a local celebration. They asked us to buy them a round of drinks, and we did; but out of the corner of our eyes, we noticed that a bottle of Couvassier, an extremely expensive cognac, was brought in on a tray but thought nothing of it at that time. We admired the traditional dress, and the students offered to bring someone to get our measurements for the dresses the next day. He arrived, did measurements, and then quoted a price and stated that he needed the money before making the dresses. It was our first day in Ethiopia, and we had no clue yet what was reasonable. After a short period of time, they requested another round of drinks. My friend and I looked at each other and decided we'd best check and see what the bill was thus far. The bill was the equivalent of over $200, and all we had had to drink was two very cheap beers. Red flag. What was going on here? The Couvassier was a big portion of that bill, and at this moment, we were at their mercy, paid the bill, which was half of the cash we brought with us to Ethiopia, and exited with all of them bantering at us. We were actually quite frightened because we were in a strange neighborhood and there weren't a lot of taxis going by. We did finally get back to our "backpacker's" but felt a lot less enthused and a bit less trusting. Not only did we lose money on being charmed into buying drinks far above what we'd ordered ourselves but in addition, we never received our dresses already paid for.

We managed to find a travel agent and book a ticket from Addis to Lalibela, then Axum and back to Addis. It was a commuter plane, an old Fokker with propellers, Dutch-made from the eighties, which accommodated approximately seventy passengers, not many being tourists. I began to have second thoughts. I quite enjoy living. The plane took off, and after five minutes, we were still in the air so I settled a bit until suddenly, it came in for a sharp landing, quite a bit earlier than we anticipated. That's because it wasn't Lalibela, it was a commuter plane, and there were several stops before Lalibela and several nerve-racking ups and downs. I had sheer gratitude for the pilot at my arrival in Lalibela for the mere fact of having arrived.

Lalibela was as fascinating as I anticipated from the reading I had done prior to coming. It is known for its eleventh-century medieval underground-level rock-hewn churches. They form as a group, a World Heritage site. It was also the time of year for pilgrimages so all along the roads there were people walking to and from other villages far and near and people holed up in tiny caverns within the church walls. People had often walked from extremely long distances to do the pilgrimage. There was a series of eleven churches, all well-preserved and still being used for the ancient services. The churches were connected by passages. They were still used for church services, which bore no resemblance to the Catholicism that I grew up in. I formed then my own perception that we all started with the same religion so many eons ago and somehow just followed different paths because it seemed to me there was a bit of Christian and Muslim tradition both in the layout and in the rites. There were monks clothed in ragged layers everywhere, and they would show ancient books and documents and relics within the churches for a tip.

The town itself was small, with roads all dirt and teeming with people. We constantly had a circle of people around us either begging or offering us trinkets for sale. Our small hotel was extremely basic, and what stood out was the smell of urine in the bathroom. I didn't notice until the second day that when I flushed the toilet, the urine would seep up from the drain in the shower. Problem solved. I guess we were lucky just to have a flush toilet and not a hole in the ground. The staff at the hotel all dressed in dirty, ill-fitting, sometimes raggedy lab coats. They did request that we send them some new ones. People constantly asked for clothing, bags, absolutely anything we had that might be of use to them.

Axum (also spelled Aksum) was next after another unnerving plane trip. It was equally fascinating and also a World Heritage site. It is known for its field of monoliths dating back centuries to ancient times. The Queen of Sheba is rumored to have been the partner of King Solomon, and there are related tourist sites—her baths and her residence, and there is the supposed Ark of the Covenant guarded 24/7. The belief among the Ethiopians and others is very strong that it is the actual Ark of the Covenant, and much research has been done tracing the movement of the Ark. I read Graham Hancock's "The Sign and the Seal: the Quest for the Lost Ark of the Covenant" published in 1993 in which he describes the research he did over a ten-year period. It seemed to me a plausible theory and made for fascinating reading.

Axum is a sprawling town with multiple historic sites to see as well as places to sit and simply observe the life. We had breakfast in a café and watching a camel stroll by nonchalantly, and later a funeral procession. Everyone in Axum, it seemed, carried umbrellas for protection from the sun. We ate in a small restaurant where we could sit on a patio. There were several beggars just sitting up against the wall across from the restaurant. We noticed that as people finished their meal, the beggars would walk across and open a small burlap sack. The clients at the restaurant would scrape the remainder of their meal from their plate into the sack. We weren't hungry after that and scraped half our meal into a beggar's sack. The beggar would immediately go back across to the wall and start eating out of the sack. It was a sight still embedded in my memory. It makes it ever so difficult to ever leave food on my plate to be thrown into the garbage.

We returned to Addis, where we had made a reservation to the backpacker's where we stayed in the beginning of our escape. We had already paid for the additional night before we checked out the first time. When we arrived, they had no record and so I pulled out the receipt. They asked us to wait while they organized a room since, at that moment, they had no vacancies. We waited for a bit over two hours, and they pointed to what would be our room once the guests vacated. A man and women walked out of the room without luggage and left the premises. The staff took a few minutes to prepare the room. We entered to find an empty whiskey bottle still on the table and rumpled sheets. I sure didn't sleep under those sheets. We later learned that backpacker's hostels in many developing countries double for whorehouses. I suppose it wouldn't have been so much of a nasty for me if they had at least cleaned the room properly and put on clean sheets.

I would happily return to Ethiopia but not again to stay in a backpacker's. The government hotels are quite nice and not that expensive. I have had the whorehouse experience knowingly now. Once is enough.

LEBANON UNDER ATTACK

On the fourteenth of February in 2005, Rafiq Hariri, the former prime minister of Lebanon, was assassinated while in his motorcade traveling through the hotel and banking district of Beirut. The blast was felt for several miles from explosives equivalent to one thousand kilograms of TNT. Many people were killed and buildings destroyed for blocks in the surrounding area. The news impacted on all of us working in Riyadh because so many of our friends working there were Lebanese. It was a period of rising tension with Syria, then very much involved in the politics of Lebanon. Lebanon had endured a civil war from 1975 to 1990, and Syria had been involved initially to help maintain security in the country; but ten years on, there was opposition to Syria's continued presence and influence. Hariri had joined the opposition for withdrawal of the Syrian troops and was extremely popular. Many were pushing for independence and democracy. Rallies, protests, and uproar followed the murder of Hariri and many of his staff. There was the usual finger-pointing, this time aimed mainly at the Syrians.

Only a week before, a friend and I had booked a week-long holiday in Lebanon to ski. It is the only place in the Middle East where skiing is possible, and we were informed by the Lebanese we worked with that it was quite a decent resort for skiing. We were still working in Saudi Arabia at the time, and it was only a short flight from there. After the terrorist attack, we had second thoughts but finally came to the conclusion that the event had already occurred and it was probably better to go there than anywhere else. The likelihood of something like that happening again so soon was almost nonexistent. We felt no fear, only some anticipation of what we might encounter.

Before the bomb blast, Lebanon had become a popular tourist destination for those working in Saudi Arabia. There were many Lebanese working in Saudi, and they were patriots extolling the beauty and virtues of their homeland. The central area had been redesigned after the civil war in Lebanon and was a charming area of trendy bars, restaurants, and boutiques. The city was as interesting as we were told, but in addition, we had the experience of seeing a country grieving and demonstrating its patriotism, much like the Americans did after the September twin tower terrorist attacks. We arrived to a country totally void of tourists. On our first full day, we wandered along the sea to the area that had been bombed. When we arrived close to the scene of the carnage, we were immediately confronted by a CNN reporter from Turkey who requested an interview. His first question was "How does it feel to be the only tourists in Beirut?" and, looking around, indeed we were. His second question was" Are you worried to be here at this moment with all the protests and tensions?" And our response was "No." It is difficult to describe the feelings I had, but it definitely wasn't fear. It was more of a desire to feel what these people were feeling at this moment and to actually participate in those feelings.

There was an area of open ground much like a very large school playground where memorials had been set up for Hariri and his associates who had also been killed. There were poster-size photos of those slain in front of what looked like a grave covered in flowers and wreaths. There was a long queue of somber people slowly making their way forward to view the monuments and have a moment in thought. There were tents set up everywhere on the grounds with thousands of people, young and old, milling around. There were young people sitting around fires, deep in discussion. There was a sense of gravity, stillness. It was peaceful. And everywhere, the Lebanese flag could be seen—the red and white flag with a cedar tree in the center.

People invited us to sit with their groups and hear their conversations, their feelings, their passions and also peak their curiosity as to why we were there. Once again, a reporter, this time from a local station, requested an interview; and we obliged him. The interviews were never about the politics, always about the feelings of being there at this point in their history. I remember just getting into the passion of it all simply by observing and sharing time with these people who were experiencing something I never had experienced. I wanted to be wherever there was a rally, wherever there was a procession of cars, all with a full-sized flag trailing outside the windows. I suppose the closest I had been to something like this was the Vietnam protests in the sixties. I couldn't help feeling the same shock and anger and desire for something better that they were feeling.

Life appeared to be going on as normal in other areas of the city. We visited the university area, and students were sitting about in the restaurants and cafés. Students could be seen carrying their books and going to classes. People went in and out of small shops and groceries with their purchases. The trendy central area was crowded with young people dressed in stylish colorful clothing. Some couples were holding hands and looking at each other with lust, others in intense conversation, solving the world's problems, much like we do on an evening out on the town.

In other areas of the city, the scars of the civil war could not be missed. I don't remember many buildings in older areas that were not riddled with bullet holes. I remember thinking at the time that a whole generation of children never knew what it was like not dodging bullets or living a normal life like children should lead, no time when there wasn't the thought of having to leave the country for safety's sake to survive. I thought how very privileged I was to have grown up somewhere where I could learn and play with the worst trauma being I couldn't do or have what I wanted. I thought how much those of us who have been lucky enough to escape that kind of trauma take it for granted. I honestly wanted to remain there and take up their cause, and maybe now I understand better why some people do that.

We were advised on several occasions to leave the city because more rallies and protests were imminent and the possibility of violence was present as is true whenever groups gather and especially when the element of anger is present. We did consider staying for just that but after all, we'd actually come on holiday to ski and so we left for Farayya, only a little more than an hour from Beirut. We followed a trail of cars with people hanging out of the windows, holding up the full-size Lebanese flags. I hung out the taxi window myself, trying to get photos. The atmosphere was electric. We turned off to the mountains, and I hated leaving the parade of cars going north to Tripoli. The scenery made up for it as soon as the mountains came into view. For a few days, the beauty and my love for snow-skiing took over and released me from the intensity of the politics of Lebanon. Farayya was not Vail or Aspen, but it was mountains and beautiful white powder without the crowds of Colorado, and that was a change from the arid, hot climate of Saudi Arabia. We walked and played and skied in the snow, conversed with the locals and for a brief period, forgot the intensity of where we had been, and just left behind in Beirut. I will say though that I did not enjoy using a tow rope once again. I've been spoiled by gondolas and triple super-speed chair lifts. Our hotel room was as basic as basic could be, and the heater was not adequate. It was cold!

We left for Tripoli north along the west coast and then spent a day skiing at Cedars. The drive there was incredible with winding roads through tiny mountain villages. We visited the house of Kahlil Gibran, who wrote *The Prophet*, an inspirational book originally published in 1923 and one I carry with me wherever I go to live. It was one of the surprises on this adventure because I never actually knew from where he had originated. The house was just there in the last town where we exited the bus to catch the taxi up to the ski area. The ski area was even more basic than Farayya. There was a single-chair lift, and I noticed everyone taking off their skis before getting into the chair. I did the same though I didn't understand the concept. In most places, one skis off the chair. I was nervous the entire ride up, wondering how I would get off but watched the people in front of me. They just jumped and ran down the steep little off-ramp. I tried to emulate the same action and fell off the chair instead, rolling down the ramp and getting out of the way before the next person jumped off.

I gave up downhill skiing after that one run; there was no way I would humiliate myself on that lift again. I cross-country skied my way approximately five kilometers back to our lodge and passed the famous Cedars of Lebanon. That was a joke. It was a single large impressive cedar; all the others had been cut down, died or whatever. But there were still many small stalls along the road selling carved items from the cedar trees. Hopefully, there were more cedars in other parts of Lebanon. Otherwise that lone large one didn't have much time left on the earth.

Our last stop was Baalbek, a city known for its Roman temples, the largest, noblest, and best-preserved of the Roman Empire. As the infrastructure of Lebanon has not developed as quickly as totally developed countries due to ongoing tensions and strife, the road system is not fantastic so we had to return to Beirut and then find our way eighty-five kilometers northeast toward the Syrian border. We so would have liked to go to Syria as well, but something in my head told me that this might not be the best time. Many of the Syrian troops were leaving Syria in response to the recent crisis, and we shared the road with them. We caught a small bus that held ten people, and the driver said they were going all the way to Baalbek. He stopped halfway and announced he was going no further; it was too late and would be dark soon. So we stood for two hours wondering what we would do next if there were no other buses. Eventually, another arrived, and we did make it in just after dark and in time to find a hotel.

The temples in Baalbek are an awesome sight at night, lit up from within. The temple compound was vast and could be seen from anywhere in the city, but the best view was from a restaurant a few stories up in an office/shops building. The temples were more worth seeing than the Roman Forum or other Roman sights I'd seen in other countries. The town went at a normal pace with no evidence of the disaster that had impacted on Beirut. It seemed just another day there.

So it was back to Beirut for a night and then a return to Saudi Arabia the next day. Things appeared to be a bit less intense upon our return, but there was really no time really to get back into the political scene. There was still a lot to be cleaned up, both in terms of the physical damage and in the hearts and minds of the Lebanese people. To this date, there is not an answer as to who caused the carnage, and tensions remain high in that region.

Motorbike Men
(Really Boys)

Now if you're reading this book front to back rather than picking out short stories, you realize that I'm a woman of "mature" age. At least that's how I'm presented to the groups I go out to when I'm working in a project, and if anyone reads my job history, they just know. The issue for me is that in my head, I'm still only thirty. And believe me, it does get me into odd situations at times. I suppose I should look in the mirror each day to remind myself of my age; but on the other hand, I'd be missing out on a hell of a lot of fun and experiences and I would have missed as well as the great friendships I have with a lot of folks younger than me. I look at the youth who can still laugh at themselves and play and think, *Why would anyone give that up to "act their age"?*

I've been on the back of many a motorbike in my travels, picked up by some young thing and didn't say no. I love that feeling of the wind in my hair, dodging in and out of traffic, whizzing along, leaving the cars stopped in the traffic jams. The things can be parked anywhere so it is right up to the front of the queue. You can wave to everyone as you pass. I always feel like a bit of a princess on the back. I can see everything and everybody and shout out to happy people who always shout back unless they started the shouting. I never worry a bit when I'm on the bike. I suppose it is a risk, but I would choose that type of demise that rather than to be sitting on a couch watching the television with a glass of sherry in hand.

I had one such adventure in Katmandu, the capitol of Nepal. I went to trek the Annapurna, one of the two main trekking adventures in Nepal (the other is Everest), and had organized at the airport with a tour director for the hotel. There are hundreds of tour guides at the airport waiting to capture the young folks who come off the plane with their backpacks and no previous arrangements made. He agreed to send someone to meet me at the hotel later to make all the arrangements for the trek. The young man came at the appointed time, suave and dressed well in a suit. We probably spent two hours over a cup of coffee, deciding the length of time for the trek, teahouse arrangements each night along the route, the bus to Pokhura and then a flight to a village, where I begin the trek of eight days returning to Pokhura. Once all the decisions were made, he asked if I would like to go visit the Swayambhu Stuka, one of the holiest of Buddha sites in Nepal that evening. The next thing I knew, I was on the back of his motorbike.

We weaved through the pedestrians, motorbikes, and cars down the tiny roads just before sunset. The streets were crowded with people, and shops were all along the route, selling the traditional tourist items and jewelry. There were fruit and vegetable markets, bars, and restaurants. It's an extremely colorful and busy city. We started a climb up the hill to the stuka, about three kilometers from the center of Katmandu. The stuka is over two thousand years old and a World Heritage site. It is situated on top of a hillock, and from one aspect, Katmandu lies below. The stuka is linked to a belief that the Katmandu Valley was formed out of a primordial lake. It was a large site and seemed a maze of buildings with many nooks containing a variety of Buddhas representing many aspects of life.

We wandered around the grounds at sunset; and it was magic, especially when the twinkling lights of Katmandu became visible down below. I stood there mystified for what seemed like an eternity. The magic spell was broken when the young man started to show his real intentions. He came close and put his arms around me and tried to kiss me. Naivety on my part once again. Thought he just wanted to show me Katmandu. The pushing of hands off and explaining that I was far too old for him began. He was persistent and didn't quit easily; but in the end, I prevailed. He didn't leave me stranded up on the hill like what has happened in other places. I breathed a huge sigh of relieve when I reached the hotel and prayed the guide for the trek would show up the next morning, and he did. Funny, even with the minor glitch, I loved the experience and found it nice that for a second, I felt desirable, even at my age.

And how quickly we can forget? I traveled two years later on my own to India, another respite from working in Saudi especially during Ramadan, no plans, only that I wanted to travel on the Indian trains and I wanted to visit the Taj Mahal in Agra. I flew into Mumbai where the fun began. I had decided on a backpacker's hostel selected from "The Lonely Planet Guide." The hostel wasn't the problem, but getting there was. I was immediately surrounded by a barrage of men, all wishing to lead me to my hostel. I refused, but one remained persistent and stayed with me as I started making my way. He led me into a hostel where I waited for quite a long time, only to find it wasn't the hotel where I had made reservations. I did eventually find the right place. This seemed to happen with great frequency. It seems that they get a small cut if they bring you into a place, whether it's a shop or a hotel, so you can find yourself constantly steered away from your destination.

It happened again when I was going to the rail station to buy my train ticket for Agra. The bicycle cab stopped at several different tourist agencies rather than take me to the rail station as I had directed. I finally jumped out and walked the remainder of the way. I found myself getting quite hostile at times, not in my nature. Every time I stepped out on the street, I was hassled to go here, there, and everywhere or to buy this or that. The negative I find when traveling alone especially in a country as intense as India is that there's no one immediate to share the frustration of that so the hostility comes out instead.

I left on the train with the hordes the next day, but it wasn't as chaotic as I had anticipated. I was in second class and in a two-bedded berth, comfortable and quiet. I arrived in Agra the next day to the same hassling and chaos as had been prevalent in Mumbai. And as exquisite as the Taj Mahal was, I was beginning to think I just wanted to call this whole thing quits. I was not coping well with the constant hassling. And as much as I have traveled and eaten off of food stalls everywhere in the world, the gut started rumbling and the trots followed. I was miserable but took my Lomotil—always come prepared—and caught the train next to Jaipur, commonly called the "Pink City."

Jaipur is the capitol of Rajasthan, a state in India and a city of over six million people. The mix is Hindu and Moslem, and when I arrived, both were celebrating their religious holidays; they just happened to fall during the same week in this particular year. It is a popular city for tourism in India due to the many historic sites. It was a walled city; and in the center, all the buildings are pink, hence the name. The old city is extremely congested normally but was even more so with the revelry of the holidays. The bike cab driver who took me to my hotel also invited me to spend the actual holiday evening with his family and be a part of the celebrations. We went from house to house sampling all of their food delicacies made traditionally for the holiday. It did remind me of my own Christmases when I was young, with the houses decorated in twinkling lights and the sharing of food and gifts. He became my tour guide for the next few days, and some days, his wife accompanied us. There was only the request for money and for gold to be put away for their daughter's future wedding plans.

On my last evening, I went through the financial district for a walk and some quiet since it was away from activity and people. I saw a rooftop restaurant that looked fairly empty where I could have a simple meal and some wine. Up I went and sat down and ordered. There were only a few tables with businessmen chatting. I was enjoying the view and my own thoughts when a young man asked if he could join me. The usual line was "I want to practice my English." The peace and quiet was short-lived. He was an interesting conversationalist, and his English was very comprehensible. We discussed education, politics, not the usual trivia so I didn't mind. And he had a motorbike!

We left on his bike a couple of hours later, and he invited me to his place for coffee. Now that does sound like a line. He worked in a bank and was well-dressed so I was quite surprised when I saw his apartment. It was one room the size of a large closet with nothing in it but a burner for boiling water and floor cushions. He had some shelves with books, but that was it. I thought that even when I backpack, I have more than that. He took me flying on the back of the motorbike, through the massive crowds celebrating in the town center, through the streets of the "Pink City," and finally back to my hotel.

Thank God, I still had a high from the motorbike because the next day, I caught the bus from Jaipur to Delhi. There are two levels of buses, one for the locals, which is very cheap, and another first-class bus for travelers. I checked several times to assure that I was buying a ticket to the first-class bus and told yes, the crowd waiting looked very local, and they were all men. The bus arrived, and we were packed in like sardines. It stopped at every little stop possible and eventually arrived in Delhi. I was indeed on the local bus; I suppose that added to the adventure.

Delhi was more chaotic than all the cities I'd traveled through in India. By then, I was quite ill with the gastric bug so instead of finding a hostel, I went straight to a four-star hotel with the intention of spending the next twenty-four hours in bed taking care of myself. In addition to not feeling well, I needed some quiet time and I needed to reenergize. I read and slept and simply enjoyed the peace, but then it was once again time to hit the streets and see the capitol before I returned to Mumbai and then home to Saudi. I read in the "Lonely Planet Guide" that a frequent ploy by young boys on the street earning a bit of money shining shoes was if you said no, they would drop feces on your shoes, at which point you would agree. I chuckled when I read it. I went out in the morning and was no further than a block from the hotel when I had shit dropped on my tennis shoes. What a humiliating experience that is. I ran back to the hotel rather than give the little shit the work.

There were no motorbike rides offered to me in Delhi, but I'm sure that wasn't the last time I'll jump on one. I'm just waiting for another adventure and another offer.

Return to a Special Country—Tunisia

I try not return to places I've lived or been to before, no matter how much I love a place, simply because there are so many countries still to visit. Tunisia was the first developing country I had lived and worked in. I was there with my husband who was involved in a National Science Foundation grant and our children who were then three and five years old. Both did their first year of school there. It was in the seventies, and there was only a small expatriate community of approximately two hundred people from many countries around the world. We all knew each other and socialized with one another;it was a very closeknit community. I loved the country, the culture, learning French, and all our newly acquired friends. Very unfortunately, we were called back to the U.S. after a year. I have always felt like I never really said good-bye because we were on the plane within the week we learned we were leaving so I never had the chance to do an adequate separation. I have for years had a yearning to return. Riyadh was only two hours away so it was my final and favorite holiday while I still worked in Saudi.

The county is tiny and located between Libya and Algeria in North Africa on the Mediterranean Sea. It is primarily Muslim but had been a French protectorate until the 1950s when it achieved independence. There remain remnants of the French influence like the reasonable wines, wonderful baguettes, and a Catholic cathedral on Boulevard Habib Bourguiba. Tunis is the capitol with a population of close to one million. Arabic is the primary language, but most Tunisians are fluent in French as well. Though probably not as well-known as Morocco, Tunisia is a popular holiday destination for

Europeans. While Saudi Arabia is fundamentalist and rigid, Tunisia is open, laid-back, and accepting.

I think returning to some place you have spent a significant period of time is an extremely difficult thing to do, especially when it has been a positive and happy period in your life. We have all the memories, and we really want it to be exactly as it was. Of course, it cannot be, and the longer it's been, the more changes there are. I knew after almost thirty years it could not possibly be the same. Everyone I knew had moved on long ago. There was the possibility only of the Tunisian couple who were good friends still living there. Habib Bourguiba was long dead. He was in his eighties when we lived there and had the influence that Fidel has in Cuba. My three-year-old son used to come home from his French school chanting the praises that started the school day. "Hey, hey, Bourguiba!" At any rate, a friend came with me, and I hired a car to do a trip down memory lane.

I really enjoyed the driving since in Saudi, I can't even drive a golf cart. We started south along the Mediterranean Coast to Nabuel, where the beautiful Tunisian pottery is made. There were so many more hotels, and they obscured the views. It was only a small disappointment. We continued on to Matmata, which is more central and on the Sahara desert. It is a quaint underground village and was used for the filming of the first *Star Wars*. They didn't capitalize on that, and they were only remnants in one hotel, mainly posters—no souvenirs. When I had visited in the seventies, we were taken to our rooms with candles. There was no electricity in the town then. As the rooms were underground, it was black once the lights are out, but now, there's electricity—another bit of charm gone. We went on to El Jem, the sight of an incredible Roman coliseum—better preserved than the coliseums I've seen elsewhere. When I last visited, it stood alone in the middle of nowhere, a mirage in the desert. It is still awesome but now surrounded by a proper village and tourist stalls. It doesn't have quite that same initial impact.

We stopped in Souse, again with its popular beaches, and then inland and south to Tatahouine. It was a place my husband spoke about because he did some work there, but I had never been there though I had wanted to so I did go this time. I remember hearing the roads were only sand that far from Tunis and they drove there in four-wheel drive vehicles. Now there are excellently paved roads all the way. We stopped on a mesa where you could overlook the town below, and there was a Berber tent set up with carpets. The Berber carpets are hand-woven, and a very friendly man sold me a carpet his wife had made. It was another memory; there were always the nomadic Berbers selling their handcrafted wares along the side of the road. This was the first one I had seen this time. Tatahouine is of interest because of the almost storybook-looking houses built right into the mountains. On our return to Tunis, we passed through Karouin, which is the religious center of the country. It remained much as I remembered it, with the huge mosque in the center and stalls selling wares surrounding it. What they are best known for in Karouin beside the mosque are the carpets. You can watch the women in front of the huge looms weaving.

Some of my favorite décor when I was married were the handcrafted pottery, olivewood, carpets, birdcages, and wrought iron we brought from Tunisia. My husband took most of it when he left so I suppose this trip was also a mission to find and purchase some of these items again. I was not disappointed because the handcrafters are alive and well and still doing their trade. One of the unique items from Tunisia is the blue-and-white painted birdcage crafted from curled wire and wood. It is often seen in designer magazines and occasionally in movie sets. In days past, we had one person in Sidi Bou Said that made and sold the birdcages from his shop, which was also his home. He was no longer there. We were directed to someone in Bizerte, a city northwest, and from there, we were sent to Raf Raf, yet another. It was two days of driving to find the birdcage maker, and in the end, we did. Now we could have purchased a birdcage in the souks (open markets) in Tunis, but no, I wanted one from the crafter. It's what I did in the past.

There are amazing ruins from Roman times in many different locations around the country. Carthage is the best known, and I was stunned by the extent of the excavations since I had lived there. There was only one sight at that time, and now there were four. In fact, the city was just one big excavation site and full of tourists. The mosaics are some of the best preserved anywhere, and there is the museum in Tunis where they can be seen. We went to one of the other sites two hours away from Tunis. We were unaware that it was market day, not that that should particularly matter, but it did. The market blocked the road leading up to the ruins, and it was not walking distance. Tunis itself has changed drastically in thirty years, but once out of Tunis, things appeared much as they were thirty years ago. The Moslem women still cover in white, and their faces are exposed; the men wear gray *burkas*. I wondered how they stood the heat.

I've saved the best city for last because if you see a poster of Tunisia, it will be of Sidi Bou Said. It is only a short distance from Tunis and very near Carthage. The entire city is white and blue. The houses are all white stucco with carved blue doors—some magnificent—and window trim. The central part of the city is pedestrian-only with cobblestone hills and little stalls and art shops. There is a restaurant at the top of the road where you sit on cushions and drink sweet mint tea with pine nuts at the bottom of the cup. The little beignet shop was still there. Nothing had changed. The city is unchanged. They know they have a good thing going. Why change it?

I spent a couple of days in Tunis after my friend left doing the real memory lane tour. I searched for the houses we lived in, the souks where I spent at least two days a week, the friends, the little French church I attended, the little supermarket I shopped at, and the American Embassy where we spent a lot of social time and commissary-shopping. I found the apartment in the city, which, when we lived there, had cows grazing on the front lawn. It was the end of the road before the airport. Now it is surrounded by apartment complexes and new roads, and the airport is no longer visible. There was a soccer stadium across the road where we would look down at thousands of men—no women thirty years ago—walking out after the soccer match. It's no longer there or at least could not be seen. Then again, perhaps I had the wrong apartment building. The other house was in Ezhara, and I couldn't find it or our friends. The beachfront had totally changed. The town remained much the same. The little French church I attended in Tunis no longer there or, if it was, unrecognizable. The embassy was an unkempt building. There was a new embassy in a different location, but I had no need to find it. I did find the home overlooking the sea, which was once the home of the American ambassador and where we spent a few Sundays at afternoon classical concerts. I never did find who it belonged to now.

Tunisian cuisine was always one of my favorites, and in that topic, I wasn't disappointed. Although Tunis itself had grown and had many new structures, Western fast-food restaurants weren't one of them. I fattened up on all my old favorites—*brik,* which is a very thin pastry round in which they will place an egg and sometimes tuna, fold it, and toss it in hot oil. It is messy to eat but so good; *mishwaya,* which is roasted peppers, onions, and tomatoes, chopped finely and tossed with a vinegar type liquid; couscous, the national dish served with a wonderful spicy tomato-based sauce seasoned with turmeric, cumin, cinnamon, and *harissa* pepper and has in it the vegetables in season, any kind of meat you choose, and garbanzo beans. I could stay forever for the food. I left with a cookbook.

I love the country, and it didn't disappoint me to return probably because I did anticipate changes. I did finish the process of saying good-bye, which I hadn't so many years ago, and I doubt I'll have that need to visit again, though if someone offered me a free package, I'd jump at the chance to go. Note: This was written prior to the political uprising in Spring, 2011. It was a surprise for me to see Tunisia as the first county in the region to have a rebellion.

BONDING IN BURUNDI

Another mission with another organization, in post-conflict Burundi, but this time there was no unbearable heat. We were in a village in the lush mountain region in the north of the country near the Rwandan border. I know when I was asked to go there, I didn't even know where it was. I had to find it on the map. I was knowledgeable about Rwanda and the horrific genocide that had taken place in the nineties but not of its neighbor. Burundi is a tiny country adjacent to Rwanda where genocide did take place as in Rwanda but never had the publicity because it was far more subtle and over a longer period of time. Certainly, the old feelings were still present. We were instructed not to ask the locals whether they were Hutus or Tutsis. There were some remaining refugee camps and still armed rebel groups who had not as yet signed onto the truce.

The village was fairly large with electricity powered by generator in some places. There were churches of every denomination with functioning schools. And on Sunday morning, we would awaken at five in the morning to the blaring of religious music from a speaker system from one of those churches on the next hill over. There was some infrastructure in the village, lots of tea and coffee fields, and lots of agriculture in general. Fruits and vegetables were available in season. There was even a local outside bar where expats and locals alike sat on wooden benches over a few beers, discussing issues while the local kids walked by herding their goats and cows. Daily, one of those goats never made it past the bar. Its neck was slit, and it was roasted on the spit.

The village folks were quite serious but friendly and frequently stopped to say hello. They spoke a local language, but those who had been to school were also fluent in French. They were poor, as is the norm rather than the exception in the rural areas. They had little and were dependent on our organization being there, both for jobs and for health care. Malaria was a huge problem, again extremely common in Africa. Poor mother-child health was the other.

The nearest town, seat of the local government, was only an hour away by vehicle, over rutted dirt roads. It was a fairly large town with approximately seventy thousand people. Many stock items for construction, food, and medical supplies that were not available in our village could be obtained there; so in general, it was a fairly comfortable setting. The capitol was Bujumbura, and that was only a three-hour drive. Almost anything was available there as long as you had the money to pay for it. There were multiple quality restaurants and discos, even a golf course. There were also lots of other aid organizations present, and the weekends could be quite social. The city was perched on Lake Tanganyika and looked across to the Kivu region of the Congo, where conflict was openly still going on.

Our living accommodations were not bad considering some of the places I've been since. We were in a large house with enough bedrooms so that each of us had our own with all the essentials: shelving, a rack for hanging clothing, even a desk. There were several toilets and shower stalls, though still the water came in buckets. We had a large living and dining area, bookshelves games, and a TV with an English satellite station from Dubai. The kitchen had a gas stove with an oven and a very large pantry. There were lots of walking trails up and down the hills. It wasn't five-star, but we weren't wanting for much. We had staff that washed and ironed our clothes, made up our beds, and did the cleaning and cooking.

The security levels were minimal and decreasing as groups gave up their arms and signed onto the treaty. There were armed soldiers and occasional checkpoints along all the roads; and normally, other than in the cities, no one ventured out driving at night. Curfews were reasonable, and we were able to go into the village in at least pairs. The local staff was very protective of the expats and would always warn us to stay in if they felt there was any trouble brewing.

It was the week before Christmas, and a large party was planned mainly by the locals for all of the staff. There was a manger scene with boughs and twinkling lights all around. The boom box was set up with one of the locals as a DJ. The bar was fully stocked, and the roasted goat and kebabs on sticks were to be passed around. Everyone sat around an open space in the middle of the room on wooden benches, waiting for the speeches to take place. The Africans in general love the lengthy orations at the beginning of any event. The dancing followed, and danced we all did. The African dancing is almost frenetic and hypnotic with the music from Tanzania, the Congo, Uganda, and other surrounding countries, and I've not met an African who can't dance. Somehow, the beer improved our white fellow dancing skills.

Exhausted after a few beers and continuous dancing over several hours, some of us retired and returned to the house. We sat on the patio, discussing the party and the fact that it was so nice that security was now decreased and we could feel a bit more normal rather than like prisoners. I left the others to go read for a bit, went through the usual routine of washing up and tooth-brushing, and tucked myself in bed, mosquito net in place, with my book. Thirty minutes later, I had turned off the light when I heard shouting, gunshots ringing out, and thunderous footsteps racing past my window. I dived out of my bed and spread myself flat out on the floor, not even bothering to see if there was a spider lurking there. Thoughts went through my head that this was really it this time and started praying. A few minutes later, one of our team called out an "all clear," and we straggled from our rooms one by one to find out what had happened, also fearing that someone was either dead or injured.

Two of the team, women, had continued talking out on the patio, also about how nice it was to feel safe with decreased security after the rest of us had gone to our rooms. Suddenly, two men stood in front of them, pointing AK rifles. They had apparently come through the rear gate of the bamboo fence surrounding the house. Speaking in English, they demanded to be taken to the safe. The project manager, being one of the two, calmly and quietly took out the key to the safe and escorted them. She opened the safe and gave them the little money that was left in there; all the staff had been paid the day before the party so it wasn't much. They turned to leave, picking up computers and mobile phones along the way. So far, so good. Up to now, it was protocol-perfect.

Then the fun began. The youngest of the team heard some noise and, half in a daze, opened his bedroom door as the gunmen were passing. He went into a chase, and the chaos began. One fell down the step, and the assumption was he thought that his accomplice was being pursued so turned around and fired. The bullet very luckily hit the wall but only a meter from the young fellow's head. The three in the room were all crouched down in different corners. The gunman came back in with gun pointed at the lad, again an assumption, to kill him. He found a terrified little boy curled up in the corner, unarmed, so he turned and walked out.

Up until that evening, our team simply functioned as a family. There were two of us over sixty, one in her forties, two in their thirties, and two in their twenties. Three were British, one was Dutch, another French-Canadian, and I, an American. It was a cultural mix and a full range of ages. We all spoke French to varying degrees but mainly English with each other. There were little squabbles as there are in families, and we ate the lunch and evening meals together as a family. We were quick to confront one another with our issues and even quicker to resolve the problems. All in all, everyone on the outside found us a delightful team and enjoyed visiting the project. We did get angry at times, but we each also had a sense of humor, which is essential to team functioning. We all got along, as normal, better with some than with others.

After the robbery, we gathered and started hearing the stories on what had just occurred while the manager telephoned the main offices in the capitol. People from the community began to show up: the police, the hospital director, and other national staff. They all appeared genuinely concerned and apologetic for what had just happened. Our expat doctor, who had been under earphones listening to the music in his room, never heard a thing and was stunned, so much so that he took over the role of host, bringing everyone something to drink. The guards for the compound hid behind the walls where we were all sitting in fear. They were afraid to go back to their posts as they were not armed.

We went through a catharsis of what occurred and our feelings until the wee hours of the morning. There was too much adrenalin rushing through our bodies to sleep. When we had finally exhausted ourselves, the young French-Canadian asked me to sleep in the bed with her because she was terrified, and so I did. I was a bit unnerved myself. Until that evening, our relationship was more on the side of tolerating one another, our idealism was at different stages of development.

In the morning, the local staff members were all there, not so much for the event itself but out of fear that we would leave and close the project immediately. Word spreads quickly in remote areas, not sure how, but it's quicker than in the developed world with all its communication technology. The fear was that it could mean a loss of jobs and no one was prepared to take over the administration of the health care for the region. There was the question of whether this was an inside job and the total lack of trust resulting from that. Not much work got done that day.

Later in the morning, the entire capitol management team arrived to debrief us, give us emotional support, and determine the next steps. The final decision was to evacuate for at least a short period until there was more information, some more safety measures put in place, and the team itself received counseling. At the time, not everyone was in agreement with that decision, but it was all or none; and so we left for Bujumbura. Our local staff all stood there as we drove out, some with tears in their eyes. Everyone lined the streets of the village as well. There was no cheering or hurrahs, only the long, somber faces.

A counselor was brought in, and we all started talking, one by one. We must have each shared our own story of what we were doing at the time and the feelings that engulfed us at least a thousand times. In fact, we talked so much and expressed our own personal feelings of the events so much that not one that I'm aware of has had post-traumatic stress symptoms. We moved from the talking to making a choice as to whether we would return to the project, either individually or as the entire group. Each individual was given the choice to leave if he or she felt they could no longer cope. Everyone made the choice to stay and to complete goals they had set. We met every day for a few hours and, toward the end of that week, had to make decisions regarding the project itself.

In the midst of this were the Christmas and New Year's holidays. There were parties, and we were invited along, even to parties we would not have normally been invited to. We frequently went out to a restaurant to eat in smaller groups and would sit and talk over bottles of wine for hours and relive the experience all over again. I went golfing one day with the lad who had been shot at, even though we were so far apart in age. We were even able to laugh some. Sometimes, individuals would just take space, and that was good as well.

By the end of the week, we had truly bonded through an experience. The project carried on, and individuals left at their contractual end point. Everyone has done well, many have returned to other projects, ready for whatever might occur. I think in discussions with some, we felt we would go out again to another setting, even if dangerous. The adrenalin rush was more powerful than the fear of another similar occurrence. Certainly, it didn't stop me.

Newsletters from the Congo

11 May 2008

I arrived a week ago to the village of Shadara, which will be my home for the next eight months. I had a day in Lubumbashi, the capitol of the region which is in the southern part of the Congo across from Zambia, for my briefing. I was thrilled to find out we would be flying to the village in a Cessna cargo and passenger plane. The village is very remote, and it takes three days by car and three hours by the small plane to go there. The plane is contracted for several organizations so it stops at other projects, leaving supplies and either picking up or dropping off passengers. It's not a medical plane so it doesn't deal with patients. Two of us traveled together from Europe for the same project; and by the time we reached Shadara, we had bonded. My mate is a lovely young Dutch guy with a great sense of humor and enjoys a beer now and then as do I so I knew no matter what the rest of the team was like, we'd still have fun.

I came again for a volunteer medical mission; it's a post-conflict area with the same kinds of problems that we had in the project in Burundi last year. I'll be doing outreach and going out to village health centers with a team of locals. At least this time, I have some experience, my French is somewhat improved, and the Congo is just one of those places I've wanted to go. I do really feel this kind of work is worthwhile; and even though changes happen so slowly, at the end, you can look back and see that you've helped in some kind of way.

We flew through mountains and landed on a small dirt airstrip. As we came down, we saw the whole team waiting below with balloons in the air and singing. We thought it was for our arrival; but alas, all the pomp and circumstance was a good-bye for someone from the project who was leaving.

We walked from the airstrip through the village to the project compound. It's a very small village in the middle of nowhere with dirt roads, rough brick single-room homes with thatched roofs, a small outside marketplace, a playing field, and stalls along the road selling a few local goods. People have returned and rebuilt the village in the past year, and apparently the growth has been remarkable. It's more secure now since the fighting ended and people are beginning to feel safe. There are no armed policemen walking about. They're building houses, planting crops; and the first goats are appearing.

And as for me, I'll be camping for the next eight months. This place is a lot more basic than the last one in Burundi. Most people have their own *tukul,* which is a small four-walled structure with a thatched roof and a cement floor. They each basically have a bed and one other wood stand to put things on, no shelving units or hooks on the walls and definitely no desks. There was a small house with two bedrooms. I chose the vacant bedroom because I thought there would be less of a chance of a visiting snake and because there was some solar-powered lighting. The *tukuls* had none. There are two pit latrines for the seven of us and one outside shower with cold water from a plastic tank that is filled a couple of times a day by woman from the village who carry the water up in ten-gallon plastic jugs on the top of their heads from the river about a kilometer away. I don't know how they do it. The kitchen is outside, the heat for cooking is from charcoal, and the oven is a brick structure fueled by wood.

25 May 2008

Call me Mama Kenna. No matter what our age or expatriate status, the national staff calls us by "Papa" or "Mama." I was happy to learn it was not only me because of my age. It's rather endearing. I'm finishing my second week here now, and I'm no longer afraid of the hand-sized spiders. I just walk past them; and anyway, they're unable to bite because of the size of their mouths. I haven't seen a mamba snake yet though they are around. The creatures tend to be as afraid of us as we are of them. I do check under my bed before I climb in and shake out the shoes in the morning. I don't mind the cold showers; they're great after a dusty day at the clinics. My aim still isn't right for the pit latrines so I often have wet ankles and I do still have the fear that the platform will give and I'll fall in.

I am truly in the heart of Africa and again sometimes feel as though I'm on a movie set. The nights are especially trying, and I'm not getting much sleep—yet. Our housing compound is in the very center of the village, which is a very remote village. The houses and churches back up to our fence. The noises we hear at night would wake the dead. The drums beat almost every night; sometimes it goes on throughout the night for a funeral. There's a different beat to signify the occasion. Some nights, shrieking pierces the air. I've been told that it might be a witch doctor scaring the sick out of someone or the priest performing an exorcism. The roosters begin crowing at four in the morning, and a chorus moves throughout the village. Dogs and goats wail pitifully. We fantasize that the animal is being sacrificed. One night, a dog wailed as if being beaten the entire night. The whole team was cranky in the morning, and we peeked through the fence. The dog was being stoned. When questioning the stoner, we learned the dog had eaten one of the man's chickens. We asked the man to stop, and he moved away from our fence with the dog. The Africans value the animals in a different way than we do. They're not pets; rather, they serve a particular purpose, and it's difficult for us to get around that.

My job as an outreach nurse has been fascinating. The team goes out in a four-wheel-drive vehicle over rutted dirt roads; and depending on the clinic, the drive each way is between two and four hours. Our team works with the team employed by the health minister of the area to provide care, to teach quality care, and to supervise the health center staff. We immunize children for the normal childhood diseases which can be deadly.

My team does a lot of teaching in the villages to encourage good hygiene practices and to come to the health center for illnesses. It's quite the task to convince people to use the center rather than the traditional healers for serious illnesses. Kids often die from measles or women in obstructed labor during childbirth because they go to the traditional healer first. By the time they reach the clinic, it's too late.

8 June 2008

It has been almost a month now so I know a lot more of what's happening and feel a part of the "family" now. The conflict here was with the Mai Mais who are not actually a tribe; they originally formed as a group after the Rwandan genocide for community defense against the Rwandan Hutus that came over to save their hides after the genocide was over. Since then, they have broken into local militias and have exploited the people. The rumor is that they apparently believe that bullets won't kill them. They burned villages and massacred many of the villagers, but this ended in the southern part of the Congo two years ago. People had gone out into the forest to live and are now gradually returning to the villages. They build houses out of bamboo or tall brush; and as they feel more secure, they build from the rough village made brick. Since I arrived, I have seen an increase in the number of market stalls and more variety in available goods. It often arrives on the back of a bicycle, with someone who has pedaled for several days from the capitol or some other province. The bikes are sometimes piled so high with goods that you can't see the cycler. The goods often include beer along with the other staples.

Our own goods arrive either by truck or the airplane from Lubumbashi, and food is a major topic of conversation, normally as complaints and whining. Some shipments have twenty cans of corn and twenty cans of peas, not much variety and not much fresh. We're lucky to have meat (obtained locally) two times per week, canned tuna, and the very rare egg. We have a couple of chickens and a rooster on the compound, but they act as if they are an alarm clock rather than chickens that produce eggs. We tried planting seeds for vegetables, but the soil is sandy; and this time of year, it's arid so things begin to come up and then die. Each new person who arrives is enthusiastic in planting a garden and then within weeks gives up.

The weather is the one perfect thing. It is the dry season, which means there is rarely rain, and the temperature is a pleasant warm during the day and cools enough for a light blanket at night. The clouds are rare until December. The lack of rain and light breezes leads to a lot of dust. We're near the equator so the days and nights are equal. The sun rises at six in the morning and sets at six in the evening, and it's instant. If you're not there when the sun begins to go down, you miss the sunset completely. The skies are incredibly clear at night so much so that we see more stars than sky. Our thrill—because most of us come from north of the equator—is to see the Southern Cross constellation.

As for work, we had a measles treatment tent set up in a far-away village where there had been an epidemic. During the time that people lived in the forest, they didn't receive health care and the children were not vaccinated while the conflict was going on. We're gradually immunizing all the children, but many have not been reached yet so measles epidemics are still common and deaths are related to the complications. The epidemic in this particular village is over now so we went to take down the tent and close that program. We sat in the dust under a tree with the village chief and as many villagers that we could find and made the announcement to prepare them for the closure. The guilt was immediately placed on the team for abandoning them. As we left the village in the four-wheel-drive vehicle, the entire village surrounded the vehicle and began a very angry-sounding exchange with our local staff. It was a terrifying moment, and I had that remembered image of the last helicopter leaving Vietnam when that war ended. We did leave without further incident; our local staff knows how to relate to the people and is composed of excellent and tactful negotiators.

15 June 2008

Another day in paradise, or should I say, every day is much the same for each one of us in our particular roles. The beating of the drums begins sometimes at four in the morning and one can only toss and turn for so long. There's not a sheet left on my bed, and it looks like a war zone when I climb out an hour later. I don my flip-flops and grab my flashlight to walk to the latrine, observing the ground for snakes along the way. I also need the torch for the latrine so I can see the hole and not fall in. It's very dark in remote villages like this because there's no electricity and only the surrounding forest; once the charcoal and wood fires burn themselves out at night, the next light is the sunrise.

The guard usually makes a charcoal fire to boil the water and has it ready in a thermos so the cup of coffee is next, sitting out in a half-torn lawn chair, listening to the roosters crowing, the children screaming, the babies crying on the other side of the bamboo fence. Meanwhile, our compound cat presses himself around my legs, begging for his bowl of milk. After my coffee, I get dressed, choosing from my couple of pairs of trousers and a few T-shirts. There is no real challenge here. Then I race to the office and the computer so I can check my e-mails. It is a contest between me and another woman who is also an early riser. We have one Internet line for all of us so gaining access to the Internet and Skype is a challenge. The cleaner begins the day early as well so it means that I lift my legs so he can mop underneath. Other staff begin drifting in so by the time I go back to the dining area for breakfast, I've said, "Bon jour, ca va?" at least ten times. Breakfast is a choice of one or two cereals or a dry roll baked yesterday with jam or cheese (rare) or peanut butter (rare).

I wander back over to the courtyard/volleyball court/vehicle parking lot located in front of the office where we gather each morning for a meeting with all the staff, expatriate and national. The meeting is not as important as it sounds although to most project coordinators, it is a white house briefing. It lasts approximately thirty minutes, and each team reports on their plans for the day and issues which may have come up. International and national news items which might have impact are related by those who have listened to their short-wave radios or read something pertinent on the Internet. Lastly, announcements are made—births, deaths, birthdays, sporting events. It's all in French so if something sounds critical, I ask for a translation. Sometimes, the discussion may have been for ten minutes and the translation comes to me in one sentence.

Then it's into the vehicle for the long bumpy ride to a health center. We carry satellite phones to radio the base and radio in at specific points along the route. I do my queen's wave as we pass through the villages. The kids all run from whatever they're doing to watch us pass. We cross over creeks or rivers on log bridges. Sometimes, a log will give and we're stuck for a bit. Other days, especially if there's been a monsoon rain, we get bogged in the mire. Sometimes, the vehicle is almost at a forty-five-degree angle when a rut in the road is deep. I remember four-wheel driving as a hobby. I can assure you, no more of that. Now and then, a vehicle comes from the opposite direction. As the roads are literally one lane or less with thick forest on each side, it takes some maneuvering.

We arrive at the clinic, and it is handshake time with clinic staff and with patients who are already waiting and perhaps some dignitaries of the village. It can take thirty minutes to get through that. I do not bite my nails when I'm out on a mission, and I go through a bottle of hand cleaner a week. There is no running water here, only the plastic jugs of clean water we bring and a bar of harsh soap. Everything is covered in dust. It takes another thirty minutes chatting with the health center nurse relating his woes and needs. There is also no electricity. Anything that occurs by night is dealt with by lantern light or candles. I give those people tremendous credit for the conditions they work in and are actually able to do an adequate job of it. The routine begins after that in terms of seeing all the patients waiting. It can be anywhere from fifty to one hundred, and in general, they are extremely patient standing there in the heat or the rain.

When everyone is seen, we return to the base, not having eaten or urinated for the entire day. The men of course have an advantage. They simply jump out of the car and pee in the bush. I go straight from the vehicle to the latrine and then the cold bucket shower. After that, I eat the remains from lunch. Sometimes it's not much. There's then some interchange at the office and beer o'clock follows in the evening. We eat our evening meal at around seven in the evening, cold because the cook prepared it and left two hours earlier. We chat for a bit and then head to our rooms by nine in the evening to read and relax and listen to music. Thank God for iPods. Then it's off to dreamland with the beat of the tom-toms.

4 July 2008

Almost forgot the Fourth of July holiday completely because of course, we don't celebrate it here. There was a holiday here last weekend—President's Day—and it did mean an extra day off work but no real celebration. That's not to say that in Lubumbashi, they were not having parades and speeches. I spent last weekend on R&R in Lubumbashi, and what a change that was. It is a city, and there is electricity and running water. I treasured my hot bath and reading to lamp light. I went out to a few restaurants; there is a variety. I went to the disco, which there are also a few, and enjoyed dancing to the African beat. There are Congolese with money in the city. They dress in suits and fancy dresses to go out for the evening and eat out and enjoy some drinks that cost almost as much as it does in the U.S. It is such a contrast from the rural areas. Another treat was going to the supermarket. There are several and a much larger variety of goods than in the rural areas but still not a Western supermarket. Several other aid organizations have their main offices here so it was also an opportunity to mingle and discuss other projects.

Now I'm back to work. This past week, I went double-camping. I remember the days I looked forward to camping trips—setting up a tent, sitting in front of a campfire, drinking a glass of wine, and gazing up at the stars. Since that's daily life here, camping as a break sounds more like a nightmare to me. Our outreach team went out this past week to our furthest-away health center to give vaccines and prepare them for a possible cholera outbreak. We stayed the night in the health center because of the length of time it takes to arrive there. I always dread the overnights because we carry army cots and sleep on those in the clinic. There are no showers, and the outside latrines are even less charming than those on the base. One of the local women prepares our evening meal, which is normally cassava, a root vegetable which is dried, pounded, and then boiled and served in a single common dish. It is traditionally eaten with the fingers and dipped into another small dish of sardine-sized fish, goat, antelope, or rat in some spicy tomato gravy, and it may include a dish of spinach-like leaves. A pan of water is brought around the table before and after to wash the hands. I think we must get some extra blessings from somewhere to keep us from getting sick because we all stick our fingers in the same bowls after washing them only in the cold water that may have even come from the river. The amount for the seven of us is probably what I alone would eat in a sitting (except for the rat).

The nice part of those camping trips though is the quiet. The villages are very small, which means fewer drums. Another special thing is the discussions with the local staff. Normally, they are on a very business-like relationship with us, but once we sit together to eat, they talk about everything—their families, their lifestyles, and their hopes and dreams. They are also extremely curious about us so it becomes a real exchange and friendship. In the morning, when the workday begins, it goes back to only business.

Some of the things we learned from them is they don't expect to live much past forty. The average life expectancy there is around forty-five years. Therefore, they marry very young and hope to have many children. There are in the village an equal number of both Christians and Muslims, and they seem to live side by side without religious conflicts. The Muslims in particular frequently have more than one wife. The Christians have one wife but often many other women—they can't understand why we're so prudish about it. I've been told by more than one person, "We're in the open with it. You do the same in your countries behind secret doors." They often name their new babies after an expat with whom they have worked. I have two namesakes in the Shadara region. We learn about their families and their culture and what people believe. It helps us to understand sometimes why compliance is not always present.

18 July 2008

Life here takes some getting used to. There's a lot of compromise and learning to adapt to different people, different foods, and a totally different lifestyle than normal. There are really enjoyable days, and there are those that make you feel that you would rather go back to bed and start the whole day over again.

Food, as I've mentioned briefly in previous newsletters, is one of those things that is a focal point in our daily existence. I find it most interesting that in any setting a person finds themselves in, whether a five-star hotel or in a camp setting, the chef seems to be the cocky one with the ability to hold power over everyone in the group and can often do the least amount of work. We live very remote and little variety is grown and produced here so diet becomes a focus of complaint. It's a good thing our cook doesn't understand English or we'd probably starve to death!

We can occasionally find a few eggs, a piece of goat or a scrawny chicken, a few tomatoes or onions but not much more. The food is sent to us weekly from the capitol after we've given them our request. We don't always get what we request because it's simply not always available. Whatever we receive that we all like—cheese, fruit, cereals, eggs, chocolate—disappears in a few days. We do receive a lot of tins of tuna, peas, and other vegetables, but everyone normally prefers fresh and that does come every week.

So to the chef, the poor man doesn't have a creative cell in his brain. Every day, it's plain rice or couscous with half the amount of water in it that's needed. He much prefers opening tins to cleaning and preparing the fresh fruits and vegetables or meat when available so it's tuna or corned beef, tinned peas, and corn, often in a tomato sauce. If the food order arrives with lots of cans of peas, we get peas every day until the supply is exhausted. The fresh produce rots in the refrigerator. He has total permission from all of us to go to the market and find what is available, but he doesn't. Each one of us in turn has attempted to teach him a new dish to prepare, such as pizza or quiche, and it's never made again unless we prepare it ourselves. To his credit, he does bake homemade rolls every few days, and that is his forte, especially since he must bake it in that brick outside oven over wood.

In some ways, we're terribly spoiled. A cleaner comes in every morning to make our beds, clean the floors, and take away the dirty laundry. The clean clothes appear on the shelves in a day or two, all pressed, even the underwear. This is actually necessary because since the clothes are dried on the line, there's some little fly that lays eggs in the clothing. When you wear the clothing not ironed, especially the underwear, the eggs burrow into the skin and then hatch, a rather unpleasant experience. The clothes are all scrubbed by hand in a big bucket of river water and very strong soap. They always come back clean, but holes appear quickly. Two pairs of my sandals went missing last week and showed up two days later, spick-and-span, so even our shoes are taken care of. The woman who washes our laundry is out in the sun, scrubbing and singing the entire time she's working. The iron is one of the antique heavy metal things which are heated on the coals.

And my issue has become that we have all our needs catered to so that we can concentrate on what we came to the Congo to do. Some of the expatriate staff do not pick up after themselves, do not even carry their dirty dishes to the basin provided for that. There are empty cigarette butts, beer cans, and dirty glasses and package wrappers on the ground left for the cleaner to pick up. It is terribly embarrassing.

10 August 2009

Soon I'll be off for two weeks to Namibia for the real R&R, and it won't come soon enough. It's been almost three months, and I know that each of us in turn is ready for a couple of weeks of almost normal living and a break from the "family" with whom we spend twenty-four hours a day. At this stage, we know all of each other's habits and most are quite comfortable farting aloud and sharing the gritty details of even the most intimate details of their lives. There are no longer any secrets. The confrontations have been few and far between, and the anger, short-lived.

I sleep well at night and don't even hear the drums beating anymore. Our chef is still with us. A few days ago, he brought a chicken from the market, and one of our mob walked in to see him killing the chicken by dipping it live into a pot of boiling water after breaking both its legs. We have all in various ways tried to demonstrate and explain more humane ways to do the deed, but it seems he thinks we're the weird ones. I suppose our ways of doing things are just as strange to the Africans as theirs are to us.

We enjoy our leisure time and play a lot of games. Volleyball and *petanque* (a French game similar to British lawn bowling) are the favorites during the daylight hours. Scrabble and various card games are played in the evening. On the weekend, we sometimes go on hikes up into the surrounding hills. We have finally honed some gardening skills and have both sunflowers and lettuce peeping through the earth. We even have a compost pile. Our compound cat is getting fatter by the day because we all spend time spoiling him. At this point, we've begun to discuss who will take him back to their home country because we suspect he will not survive after we're gone. He shall become cat stew. Some of us are making yogurt from scratch, and others are making mango wine. We do all have our different ways of preventing boredom. There are a couple of people who simply work all the time.

I spent last week recruiting a local person to fill a health educator position. It is a very basic position with a focus to educate the population in basic hygiene and prevention while they wait in line to be seen by the nurse. We had over fifty applications for the position even though it is low-paying. The applicants ranged from security guards to doctors. I became aware of how desperate people were for paying jobs. There were specific qualifications for the position, but people applied whether they had the qualifications or not. The other thing I also became aware of was some of the local corruption. We advertised the positions openly, but somehow, they were not allowed through to our gates without paying someone to pass. It was nipped in the bud when we learned of the practice.

25 September 2008

Namibia now seems ages ago and only a dream. It was lovely to see real infrastructure and a proper city with good paved and maintained roads. There were shopping malls and trendy clothes to purchase. There were lovely hotels and restaurants and a city-center small park where the African schoolchildren dressed in traditional costume performed dances. And throughout Namibia, there were game reserves with the animals in the wild. There are very few animals, mainly monkeys and antelopes left in the Congo. Presently, those are killed and eaten. The pillage of war has not been kind to them so one must go to Namibia or South Africa or Tanzania or Kenya or Botswana to see the big five—lions, elephants, giraffes, hippopotamuses, and zebras. The two weeks restored my energy and spirit for the few months I have remaining in the Congo.

Rainy season has come in with a bang, seemingly a bit early. We started this past Monday with a very calm day. We had a visitor from the capitol, to whom I was giving a tour of the hospital later in the afternoon. The sky had become quite dark, and we had debated whether or not to go. The hospital is across the main road from the office and housing compound. In the end, we went. We were no farther than the hospital entrance when the high-speed winds suddenly gusted with force and was followed with pelting heavy rain. It was immediately followed by hailstones the size of marbles. Within minutes, there was an inch of the hail collected on the ground. Thunder and lightning joined in.

The hospital is a series of small buildings with corrugated metal roofs and large tents for the tuberculosis patients, the maternity patients, and overflow. All the cooking and dining areas are open areas with thatched roofs. The metal roofing started flying. Tents were toppling. A very large tree fell into the tuberculosis tent. It all happened extremely quickly, and everyone was running for shelter. Thankfully, there was quick thinking and action by our expat water sanitation person and a Congolese doctor. They ran from tent to tent, ignoring the painful pelting of the hailstones and took all the patients who were in the tents to the safety of the brick structures. No one was injured though when the total assessment of the damages was visualized. It was a miracle. The entire storm lasted approximately one hour, and after it was over, there was debris everywhere. Trees were down, part of the roof covering offices in the main hospital was gone, and the records stored there were soaked with rain. Very little of the bamboo fence surrounding the grounds was left standing.

The housing compounds suffered much less. Large sections of the fence were gone so we looked right into the village houses surrounding us—a chance to know our neighbors? Amazingly, all the staff had remained calm and followed all the protocols. The communication system was shut down until the lightning stopped and then the main office in the capitol was notified after it was over and the initial assessment was done. A complete assessment wasn't done until the next morning because by the time the storm finished, we were in total darkness. The patients were all accounted for and placed in empty hospital beds in the main structure.

Another remarkable thing about the event was the speed and efficiency with which everything was cleaned up and repaired. We were up at daylight to take photographs and make a final assessment. By the time we arrived, all the hospital staff and village people had begun and were working feverishly at the cleanup process. By the end of the day, everything was functioning, and by the end of the week, back to normal. We're calling it our "Tempest." Rainy season is well and truly upon us now. The sky turns black and threatening every afternoon now, and we normally get a fifteen-minute downpour. It means we have a lot more little insect creatures, and soon, I may have the privilege of seeing a scorpion in the wild.

6 October 2008

I've spent a fair amount of time on the road the past few couple of weeks, both visiting clinics and doing exploratory missions to see if there are people out there who need health care and have no access to it. There was also a rumored cholera case. In one sense, I say each day is the same, but in actuality, the work may be but what we see changes every day. We have no idea what we might meet on the road or in the health centers. Since the rainy season is here, so sometimes are cholera epidemics. We keep our ears and eye open because the disease is deadly if not treated immediately. It is a disease transmitted by feces wherever it may be, and here, it's often in the water. People often get their drinking water and bathe in the rivers, the same place where they often eliminate their feces. Aside from identifying cholera when it strikes, we're here to teach the population better hygiene for prevention. It is a form of severe diarrhea so the feces pour out nonstop. As fast as fluids go in, they come out so if not treated, dehydration occurs and leads quickly to death. Since it's transmitted in the feces, isolation procedures are necessary to keep it from rampaging through an entire community.

We left Shadara and drove an hour to the nearest health center. Lo and behold, a woman with suspected cholera lay on a mat and feces surrounded it. She was dehydrated and barely responsive. An IV had been started, and the staff treating her was wading in the wet mire in their sandals. We called for a vehicle to pick her up to take her to the hospital cholera isolation tent; there was none available. We had to quickly teach everyone the protocols for isolation and treatment and protecting themselves. They had been taught the previous year, but it seemed a review was in order. The patient was later taken to the hospital and did survive. There were no further cases in that particular community.

Our next stop was dropping off several of the outreach team members at a river crossing to attend a meeting on the other side in Pweto, a larger town where the Ministry of Health for the region is located. We arrived to find the bridge in disrepair and unsafe for crossing. This is a frequent occurrence in the underdeveloped countries in Africa. We probably could have crossed in a four-wheel drive through the water, but it wasn't approved by our organization due to the risk so our guys simply rolled up their pant legs and skipped across over the rocks. We sat for two hours in the blazing sun, waiting for the vehicle to pick them up on the other side. We then headed off to the next community three hours later than planned. We arrived in time to set up for the evening, too late to begin anything else.

There was a woman in labor. Babies are born in the local health centers unless there's been some notable complication. Some clinics have midwives, and others, just the local village woman who performs the deliveries. The delivery room is just a small room with a birthing table, covered with only a plastic sheet, and a desk covered with everything from last year's paperwork to a sterile delivery pack and a roll of filament to tie off the umbilical cord. There was a bucket of water and a bar of soap and gloves, but no gowns to cover. And there is no fancy equipment to monitor the baby's heartbeat. It was dark by the time the woman was ready to deliver. I went in to assist and found the birthing attendant working with only a dim Chinese kerosene lamp that often flickered down to nothing and a candle. I assisted by holding my own head lamp where she was working so she could see what was happening. I guess if I was to come back as a midwife in Africa, I'd need the eyes of a bat. A healthy baby was born without any pomp and circumstance, no fancy anesthesia or spas, and all went well. I might point out though that when there are complications such as an obstructed labor, the woman is often brought in to the hospital on the back of a bicycle, and that could take hours. I can't even fathom dealing with that as a woman.

Another day on the road and another health center, I was setting up to vaccinate the children under a tree. A mother came to me with her half-dead baby; it appeared malnourished and unresponsive. No sooner had I assessed the baby when a man from the village came to take me to look at his daughter of four years who had been bitten by a snake a couple of hours earlier. He had done the right thing and wrapped a compression bandage above the bite area and the child appeared fine at that moment. We closed shop and loaded everyone into the vehicle for the three-hour journey back to the hospital. Along the way, we collected another patient, this time a woman in labor with complications. This was not a totally atypical day.

The journey back was hell in the heat, with the vehicle packed full like sardines, no drinking water left. We listened to the driver's old religious music tape playing over and over until I wanted to scream. And I may have screamed once out of the vehicle and earshot of everyone else.

18 October 2008

I came face to face with a twelve-inch black emperor scorpion this past week, and I'm still here. I stood up and started walking to the latrine when I noticed the scorpion slowly moving toward me. I was hypnotized and just stood there and stared while it continued toward me. I was told that scorpions can hypnotize you with their eyes; it certainly did me. I had called out "Scorpion!" when I saw it, and the others I was with broke the trance by shouting at me to run and so I jumped up on the nearest chair. Meanwhile, the guard came running in with a board and clubbed it to death. Shame, it was a proud creature; my immediate impression was of a black lobster looking me straight into the eyes. The scorpion's look is far fiercer than its bite. The sting is painful but normally not fatal to an adult. I'm glad I didn't need to find out.

We did have a security incident this week which made us all a bit more aware of where we are. While this region seems very tranquil and we rarely see military or police presence, the conflicts have once again escalated in the north in the Kivu region. We listen to the news daily to keep abreast. Last week, I was out on the road again to our furthest away health center when I received a call from the base. One of our other vehicles was stopped by armed policemen unknown to us; they were looking for a particular local staff member, and he happened to be with us. Another vehicle would come and meet us so that we were traveling in a convoy for safety. We were all tense as we drove back. I think my young male mate was more terrified than I was, but then age helps. We made it back without further incident. There have been armed police in the community off and on. They come in and drink with the locals expecting this for free and then often get drunk. We heard a gunshot one night at midnight and learned the next day that two of them were drunk and began fighting. He was trying to kill the other but luckily missed. No one was hurt but we're more reluctant now to wander out at night when we hear they are in town. I guess it's not so tranquil and secure anymore, and we do wonder if any of the conflict in the North will extend down here.

Lastly, we've had a changing of the guard. When one person arrives and another is leaving, the local staff expects, actually demands, a leaving party. The person leaving is expected to buy a couple of goats and enough beer for each person to have two. They organize the music and speeches. The formalities of course went on for over an hour before the music began and then lasted until three the next morning. The Sunday after was very quiet.

16 November 2008

If you watch international news, you've probably heard that things are continuing to escalate in the Kivu region in the north. The rebels are on the loose, and people have been massacred. Many of the aid organizations have evacuated, and some of the towns are being held by the rebels. Goma, the capitol of the region, is apparently a nightmare with thousands of refugees seeking shelter. It remains peaceful here with nothing more than the occasional armed military passing through. Our expat team huddles in a group having our morning coffee or tea, listening to the news on the satellite radio each morning before we start the work day.

There are still many things to focus in on here. The rainy season is in full swing, and with that all the activity comes with rain. The insects, snakes, and scorpions come out of hiding and make their presence known. One of our team found a strange little worm like creature wiggling on the floor in his *tukul* (the single-room houses each staff had as their room). It was the second one he had seen. On closer inspection by one of the locals, it was deemed to be a baby black mamba snake. The adult bites are extremely deadly within hours. A few days earlier, he had heard a hissing sound while having a siesta. The nest was never found. I came back from the field one day to see a few of the local staff on my roof. I later learned that they were doing repair on the roof when a green mamba slithered out and across to an overhanging tree branch. That snake wasn't captured either. Another morning at coffee, our doctor told us we had all better start wearing closed shoes and carrying our torches at night. He came back from the hospital late and went into the kitchen for a snack. A mamba was curled up on the floor, and he had almost stepped on it. Earlier the same evening, I went to the kitchen for a drink and heard rustling up in the plastic sheeting covering the roof. I did leave the kitchen quickly. I'm happy to be leaving soon, not thrilled about so many mambas around. It is surprising that there are not more bites amongst the locals because they do wander through the forest.

We now get sudden severe storms every afternoon with thunder, lightening, gale force winds, and pounding-down rain. They never really last that long, normally an hour or two. It means running around and closing all the windows, moving all the chairs and other paraphernalia under shelter, and basically stopping anything else we're doing. A few nights ago, we had all retired and were in our own rooms when there was a very large crashing sound. We were all outside instantly in various stages of nudity. The largest papaya tree had fallen over and just missed one of the *tukuls*. Our guardian angel was there that night for sure. It was old and hollow on the inside.

This is the last letter from Shadara. It's been seven and a half months now, and in three weeks, I will be on a plane to Lubumbashi and then back to the States. I have very mixed feelings about leaving. I look forward to seeing family and friends. I look forward to a Christmas as I know it and to all my creature comforts. The sadness is, and each person who has done a project like this feels the same, that we have spent the time creating a working relationship with many of the local people and are on a trust level with them. We've put some changes in place and normally seen some positive changes and a small improvement in their quality of life. They have to get used to our various French accents and adapt. They have to go through this process all over again, every nine months. We simply return to our home countries and slide back into normality. And of course, we say good-bye to a lot of new friends whom we know we'll never see again.

SERVICE OR SELF-SERVING?

Off I go again to another crisis somewhere in the world. For me, it's been mostly to Africa for an epidemic, for malnutrition, for post-conflict medical care, always with an organization and mostly on the spur of the moment. When I mention to people I meet that I work for a volunteer medical organization, mostly in Africa, though it could be wherever else there's a need, I often get the bows and the hugs or handshakes and the "Bless yous" and the "I couldn't do it. Thank God for people like you."

The guilt suddenly takes over, and I feel like a scam artist. Granted, the conditions can be quite harsh, and the living, even harsher. The houses for aid workers are right in the middle of some of the most remote areas, and it's sharing with a bunch of normally very unlike people, not only in age and culture, but also in tidiness, flexibility, habits, and ability to communicate and just be part of a team. The cook is always local and often knows how to make one or two dishes and so variety is not the name of the game. The food is usually what's available locally and often, "that ain't much." Some of the foods that get put together in the same dish are beyond belief—sardines in a spaghetti sauce, tuna in a dessert, can't even recall some of the combinations. And if there's a can available, why use the fresh stuff? It takes more time. The toilets are often outside and are holes in the ground, though it is good crouching for those pelvic floor muscles. The problem is there may only be one for ten people, and guess what, they all start with the work at the same time. The showers are mostly cold and sometimes just buckets. You can boil pails of water over the charcoal if you need that hot shower, but again, there's always that queue.

The work days are always long, and the work is never really done. The local staff somehow does not acknowledge time off whether it's because they don't have any or because they don't have the ability to delay gratification. Leisure time is only therefore when you have a moment or you go and hide somewhere no one knows about. Normally, that only place to hide is in your bedroom, if you have one of your own. When it's a real emergency, privacy is not a high priority. Socialization is often sitting down and having a beer with colleagues (if you're not in a strict Muslim country) and talking, which inevitably turns back to work issues. It tends to lead to two separate groups, one which sits and never stops talking shop and the other which carries on about anything and everything and often solves all the world problems.

I have no clue how people who are not interested in reading get by because options for other activities are limited. I have found that most who end up doing this kind of work are voracious readers and the libraries end up being wonderful. Everyone comes with as many books as they can carry and then each gets passed around and they all get left behind. You can tell how long a project has been in motion by the size of the bookshelves. Sometimes there's a Scrabble or a Trivial Pursuit and always decks of cards. In one project, we had a French *petonque* set, a bit like bowling with small lead balls being thrown around the compound, as a bit of competition. Sports are always a winner so somehow the volleyball net is always present. Internet of course is hit or miss, and if it's a hit, once again, there's a queue. And let me tell you, this is where real ugliness comes out—someone hogging the computer when there are ten other people waiting.

Curfews are often in place, and usually it's home by dark or, if not so rigid, only out with more than one and escorted by a guard. One totally loses their sense of being an independent adult. I personally feel like a child with no control whatsoever, unable to judge danger or make decisions. It places a limit on getting to know the population on a more holistic level than simply health. Sometimes, there are other organizations present in the same place and social interaction does take place. Parties do happen. The most happening parties, though, are the parties with the local staff, Christmas, or a leaving party for someone.

Well, back to the original purpose of this story and the question for me of whether it is service or self-serving. It is always a dilemma for me, and I've wondered if anyone else feels the same because this is written in retrospect. I feel very selfish in all of this. I get to go to places in the world that no one else can go, and I totally love traveling. It's my real profession after all. And it doesn't cost me anything to get to these exotic places. Granted it's not in first-class, but I've rarely traveled in first-class anyway. I get to spend several months to a year in these places and know and understand a bit about what it is really all about. I get to try really weird foods. I've eaten caterpillar and termite stew. I have R&R after a few months, and I can choose to visit neighboring countries. I have a lengthy period of time not having to hear news, particularly the political analyses of things, which gets my heart pumping. I don't have to keep up with any tedious responsibilities like attending weddings, sending birthday cards, maintaining my house, etc. I can avoid winter.

Even greater is the joy I feel when I see a bit of progress being made. I've seen malaria death rates decrease, children immunized so they won't die of measles, nutritional improvement, and more. In our country, we expect those kinds of changes overnight. There, it's over a much longer period of time, but there's the sheer looking back and saying, "We did do some good." Here in the U.S., in practice, there is often the lack of appreciation, rather the threat of a lawsuit. There, there is often not a thank you, but instead, a smiling mom showing you her improved child and a newborn named after you. It is those moments in particular that I feel a sense of pride in, and that's when I get that feeling of "I'm here for my own reasons."

I have met those who come with only philanthropic goals, but they are few and far between. Many come choosing this type of work as a career choice. Some give up making much bigger money in private or public companies in their profession. It seems to me that is selfless, though the goal is often to work toward getting into the big-time stuff like the UN or World Health Organization. The pay isn't too bad in those positions.

There are those I've met with less glorious goals. An example is the one who comes in because there really isn't any place else to go in the real world because he or she really isn't good enough given the competition. There can be a sense of power over a population that is needy, and therefore, the control instinct takes over. That too can be carried to extremes. I've seen individuals who are actually racist and quite cruel in their decision-making. It seems to me that that is totally selfish, and control freaks need to be looking elsewhere for a profession.

We can even go a step below that. There are those who come along to escape somebody or something. There was one person whom I remember who was the subject of rumors was he owed lots of money in child support and needed to stay away from his own country. Luckily, his ineptness got him out of there. I've known a few alcoholics along the day who couldn't even function at the start of the day. Luckily, that's not subtle, and they're out fairly quickly.

And there are those who probably actually do get into it with truly selfless goals but are unable to "cut the mustard." They have no realistic perception of themselves and therefore set for themselves unrealistic goals. I've seen people who have not dealt with their personal issues and carry their baggage with them, people with emotional issues, sometimes quite severe. A lot of energy then gets drawn from the real tasks at hand.

I suppose in the end, we all believe we're being selfless. Buy hey, how do we separate ourselves from our own ego and our egotistic needs? It's a balance that needs to be achieved.

Looking for Love in the Most Unusual Places

It's just another day in paradise. Each day is exactly the same. The sun is up at six, and it comes up instantly, can't watch it in wonder for a half hour. It is hot, dusty, and dirty; the ruts in the dirt roads never change. Kids run around in oversized torn clothes. Boys are even sometimes in dresses. The children chase after strangers, saying, "Donner moi" (Give me something) and hold out their hands. Each little roadside shop in the village has the same few things—tins of tuna, small boxes of tomato paste, small packets of biscuits, manioc. There's a large mosque which dominates a corner on the main road. There's a mosque in every village and small town here. The population tends to be half Muslim and half Christian. There's no running water or electricity. Occasionally, an old beat-up truck, piled high with sacks of flour and people hanging everywhere, rumbles into town. And always, there are the land cruisers of the various NGOs who come "to deal with crises—malnutrition, health care, malaria, measles, cholera, and water sanitation" then stay a while but never long enough to solve all the problems.

The kids have skinny little legs and arms and big abdomens, and many have reddish-colored hair, all signs of malnutrition. Everything in the surroundings is green and lush, and everything grows, but it's one of the poorest countries in Africa—the Central African Republic. Once, it was rich with diamonds, and then came the government rules and regulations, and many of the mining companies closed or moved out. Once, the village of Bolra was a busy place; buses came and went. Many more delivery trucks came through in the past than currently. The roads are now dusty and full of ruts. Gasoline is sold in ten-liter plastic jugs at little makeshift stands. Gas pumps do not exist there.

The houses are rough brick shacks in varying states of disrepair. There are some old colonial architecture buildings that are mostly run-down and vacated. In the past, the locals went to the river and just picked diamonds gleaming in the water and sold them to the offices of the mining companies located in the village, but that was more than two years ago. Now, the men often wander the roads, bathe in the rivers, socializing at the same time, and work in the fields, cultivating the manioc or just sit under a tree, talking. Some of the men tend to the children while their wives work in the fields.

Gloria was a young woman who arrived with a medical organization and was idealistic, as so many who arrive for the first time. She was thirty-five, Italian, and full of excitement about her new experience. She loved talking to everyone she met and most got caught up in her enthusiasm. Her French was fair, though she had an accent, but it didn't make her insecure about rambling on in French. Her joy radiated to everyone around her; and wherever she went, the local people stopped her to say hello and talk. She was positive about almost everything, and we developed a friendship from the beginning. I had arrived the week before Gloria for the field nursing post.

This wasn't the easiest project to be positive about. It seemed chaotic from the day I arrived in the capitol of Bangui. I was picked up at the airport, exhausted and feeling dirty, and barely had time for a shower before having to jump in a vehicle and travel for the next six hours to Bolra, the village described above. I arrived late in the afternoon to a very small compound with motel rooms in front of the gate. An office-come-house for the expats existed behind the fence which backed up to the motel rooms. There was someone acting in charge, and he did his best to welcome me and deal with my shock and exhaustion. I was shown to a bed in one room of the two-room office area. There was another bedroom with three beds and the only inside shower and toilet. There was a small outside patio area and a small kitchen area located on the patio. I was told things would improve; the project was just coming out of emergency mode. I had no place to unpack and make myself feel at home. Everyone was just climbing over one another and each other's things without any sense of privacy at any time.

The team was entirely made up of mainly young Spanish women in their twenties. The man who had greeted me was only there temporarily. A few spoke some English; all spoke minimal French, but in social conversation, they launched into Spanish, and both Gloria and I were then outsiders. My Spanish at that time was not even basic. Each person did their own thing in the work-related areas, and the whole project was described later by many as anarchy. Initially, there were no coordination meetings. The first couple of weeks, I noticed that everyone was working from sunup to long past sundown, and that included both days of the weekend. No one ate before nine in the evening, and then it was straight to bed. I did the same and initially had no choice. I was out in the villages with my team until just before dark, and after a quick shower and some food, I sat in front of the computer for two to three hours, often by candlelight, entering statistics from the day.

Gloria was not a medic; her job was to organize the food and supplies to be transported with the teams to the villages. She was also responsible to assist with the organization of setup of the program field, identifying problems with setup, structure, sanitation, and such things. She too worked from the wee hours in the morning until well after dark, again as most do in emergency situations. It was burning us out at the end of two weeks, working twelve to fourteen hours a day without a day off. It was eat, sleep, and work; and I seriously started thinking about leaving the project. It simply was not healthy, physically or emotionally, for anyone there. I decided to first try just no longer working on Sundays, and that did work for me. The other thing that helped was that finally a house separate from the office was obtained, and although we still shared rooms, there were spaces to go and hide. Third was just having a support person in terms of a friend. I could cope for three months.

That was the time really when Gloria and I bonded. We both needed more than just the work and 24/7 companionship of the same small group of people. We were after all in another culture, and shouldn't part of that time be spent in getting to know and understand the people a bit better? It's necessary if you want effective programs. So we began mainly on the weekends getting out and seeing what was happening in the village. We would often stop at the local "disco," where we would drink a couple of beers and eat the small pieces of roasted goat wrapped in a banana leaf with a hot curry spice to dip the goat in. And we socialized with the locals. The truth is that when they know and like you, they also protect you. If anything is in the air, they know and assure you know. It's a funny thing. There are no computers and not that many cell phones, but information travels faster than in more developed countries. And so Gloria, in particular because she was so charming, was protected and was perfectly safe to go anywhere in the village on her own. She did have many friends in the project but more often than not, they were the local staff.

I also learned a lot about Gloria on our ventures. She was single. Though she had had several relationships with men she was attracted to, nothing actually ever worked out. And she tended in the past to choose selfish men.

That burning question of "Who am I? What am I doing with my life? What's wrong with me?" was part of the reason she chose to come far away with a volunteer organization. Her father had died when she was quite young, and he had been her hero. Mom was aloof, narcissistic, verbally abusive, and never really supported anything Gloria chose to do. She had been an only child, and without a doubt, she was looking for love. She loved kids and wanted to have a child of her own. And as so many women who come to Africa to work, she did fall in love with an African man. Was she looking in the wrong places?

In the beginning, it was an incredible adventure into new territory—sex with a black man. She described it as getting back to her primitive instincts, and the sex was basic and like nothing she'd had before. And it was terribly addictive. He was married, but guilt never was an issue; it was common for an African man to have other woman. Neither really understood the other in terms of each other's value and moral system. He said to have more than one woman was normal and what was wrong for it to simply be in the open instead of lying and pretending otherwise as was the norm in Western cultures. I spent the next couple of months listening to Gloria talk about her ups and downs in the relationship. She felt she was truly in love with him and him with her. I remained entirely nonjudgmental but somehow wanted to say, "Hey, this kind of thing never works. It's a poor culture, and he wants the option to become a part of yours. Nothing more or less."

I spent a lot of time mulling over the issue of marriage between cultures, and in each working situation in Africa, there have been one or two women who become involved in a relationship with an African man, often not with anything in common, not even the career path. For example, I've seen the financial officer with a driver, the manager for the project with the local person working in the office. The expat always has the upper hand financially in these situations and in a way should have more knowledge of the relationship dynamics, but somehow, the emotions and the scrutiny seen in one's own culture seem to take over and in the end, the expat in most instances walked away in tears and the African moved on to another willing person. There was one relationship that seemed to be going very well between a female expat doctor and a male African doctor in a previous project. It lasted the duration of the project. When she left, she waited for his call, which never came. The woman sometimes just goes way overboard, and I wonder if they've taken leave of their senses. I remember an older woman (nowadays described as a cougar) take up with one of the drivers thirty years her junior. He loved the gifts she brought him and the trips she took him on to other countries and paid for. The relationship lasted three years until she found he had another relationship with one of the newer and younger expats. I've seen a lot of those types of relationships, but to date, none have remained operational. So I guess I still don't understand the thrill in it. Maybe if I was thirty again, I might. And anyway, who am I to pass any judgment?

Certainly, Gloria's relationship never interfered with her hard work. Both of us spent most of our weekdays in different parts of the region with our teams, diagnosing and treating malnutrition. Sometimes, we would find a child on death's door and return as quickly as possible with the child and parent to the hospital on base. There were the occasions where the child died on the way to the hospital or within the first few days of being admitted. Those were days when no one in the compound said much to one another. The loss of a child, no matter one you hardly know, is extremely difficult. There were times I think the staff had more difficulty coping than did the parent of the child. But the Africans keep much more hidden in terms of their emotions. Even though they've had death visit far more frequently than any of us can imagine, losing a child in its start in life leaves a total lack of comprehension. There is always the guilt in wondering if any more could have been done; but watching this team, I don't think anyone could have tried any harder. The children were simply brought to us too late.

There were also environmental factors which kept us from reaching areas where malnutrition was present. We had a program at one site that involved a river crossing. The river was more than a stream. And we reached the river the first week I was in the project only to find that we could not cross. The only way to cross was either by *pirogue* (a canoe) or a metal barge which was pulled across on cables manually by two local persons. The cable was strained and ready to snap and therefore unsafe. We were only able to see a few children whose mothers walked the three kilometers from the village and then crossed in the *pirogues*. It was well known it would be a very long time before the cable was repaired. It took months and some problem-solving. We could not cross in the *pirogues* because of the numerous supplies that we carried with us. It was food for the child and the families for a two-week period as well as the medical equipment. We did go two weeks later, thinking that the patients would cross. We arrived that time to find the river had risen even higher. In fact, it was at mild-flood stage due to heavy monsoon rains. A day earlier, a woman crossing in a *pirogue* had drowned when the *pirogue* toppled over in the strong current. It took six weeks before we could visit that village again. The mapping is not good, but we did find a road that led to the village which took a bit more time but at least we could get there and finish the program we started.

Once a week, I stayed overnight in a village. It came about because each time we went, there were more and more children to treat; and on two occasions, we had to leave to reach base before dark and left probably thirty children there untreated. We would arrive to at least a hundred mothers or fathers with their children already waiting, and as the day progressed, more and more would continue sauntering in. We returned to base frustrated and exhausted and had to find another solution. In the end, we decided to have two days in the region with an overnight. We stayed in a small typical African motel. Each room had a single cement bed covered with a thin well-used and flattened sponge mattress and a single chair. The owner brought us a bucket of water to clean up and a lantern at night. Dinner was cooked by the lone female who was on the field team. I sat with her one evening while she prepared the termite and caterpillar stew over the charcoals. I did taste it, and it was lovely; but knowing what it was put me off a second dip.

And so the three months passed. We received a new team who would carry on the program with different goals because the malnutrition had reached its peak and was in abatement. The children had many other health needs as well which we hadn't been able to address. We did receive a coordinator who was able to create some cohesiveness amongst the team, but even as I left, it wasn't a real team but a lot of very bright strong committed individuals. As forGloria, she left her man behind. She was a bit sad in the beginning but then moved on and is continuing with aid work and still as eager and vivacious as ever. Perhaps she'll meet her man yet in another project.

How Quickly Life Can Change

Le Cruz de Huanacaxtle is a little not-so-forgotten fishing village on the Bay of Banderas north of Puerto Vallarta. It's only a forty-five-minute trip to the Big Apple by car or bus, but there's an hour time difference, a thing that confuses many a tourist and new resident. It's not unusual to keep the clocks at Vallarta time because that's where everything is happening and then arrive to an appointment in Le Cruz one hour early. Businesses keep the Nayarit time.

Note: The time difference was eliminated as of 2010.

At the moment, Le Cruz is a favorite of the governor for the state of Nayarit and is being developed with a new marina on the "Riviera Nayarit." I chose to buy a house here two years ago simply because, number one, I couldn't afford Vallarta, and number two, because of the greed principle, I could only make money in a bit of time because of all the development happening. My only requirements when I was looking were that it couldn't be a condo with all the wrinkleys. I wanted young people around and a garden. Secondly, I wanted it where there were some Mexicans. If I wanted to be around Americans, I would have moved to Florida. So the house is in a gated community, and I have several lovely Mexican neighbors and a beach and marina five minutes away.

I arrived a year ago to the house and excitedly unlocked the door only to find it covered in mildew and reeking. First tasks included opening all the windows, turning on the electricity and then the gas. The first two were easy. The gas was another story. Alas, then came the neighbors. Juan and Rosita lived next door, a couple in their midsixties, neither more than five feet standing straight. Juan spoke a few words of English, Rosita, not a word. My Spanish vocabulary when I arrived was approximately five words—*hola, baños, buenas dias, cerveza,* and *adios*. It has improved now, thanks to the neighbors. Juan and Rosita went into the room where the water heater was located and fiddled, both looking at each other and making suggestions as to what the problem must be. After thirty minutes of going to and fro and exchanging glances and words, poof, the gas was on.

Neither ever stepped out on their patio without looking over and saying, *"Buenos dias y como esta?"* I loved to sit on the patio and watch the action next door. There were two hammocks, strung up horizontally to one another, a couple of inches apart. The two of them would swing in the hammocks for hours in unison and talk. Though I didn't understand a word, it was of very good friends, just chatting in a loving, warm tone. I never heard a voice raised. They did everything together, and it included a lot more than sitting in front of a television in rocking chairs all day. They would go off in their car in the morning and return late at night or a day or two later.

They did tell me a part of their story. They met when they were very young in their hometown in a rural part of Jalisco and were good friends. Juan was offered a job in California and left for the opportunity. It was where he learned some English. He was there for five years but missed his Rosita and made his decision to return and marry her rather than work his way up in the company. They had been married almost forty-five years. They had two daughters living still in the village in Jalisco.

They both loved gardening and would go plant a rosebush or an aloe vera together. I never saw them without their smiles and something cheerful to say. They asked questions and were truly interested in our responses. They asked about friends and family who had visited. They went to the Catholic Church in the square each Sunday. Juan passed the collection basket, Rosita did the readings. Rosita prepared the meals while Juan sat next to her and conversed. I could hear the chop, chop, chop of the salsa being made from scratch. It seemed to take hours for both the lunch and the dinner, and there was always the chopping.

Then one day last April, the car was packed, and they came over to say good-bye. They were returning to their home in Jalisco for several months where Juan still did work some and also to see their family. They gave us hugs, and off they went. It seemed so still after that. I missed the sounds of their talking and the hammocks swinging together. I realized I had been living vicariously in the joy of their relationship. I left two months later and was away far longer than anticipated.

I returned six months later and saw their car in their driveway but for several days heard the sounds of people talking but not of Juan and Rosita together. The hammocks were not up; there was no swinging in unison. After several days, I saw the little figure of Rosita sitting in a chair in the corner of the patio, almost hidden and smoking a cigarette. I hadn't remembered that she smoked. She acknowledged me, but not with the joy of the year past. We spoke a little, but my Spanish was rusty, and I knew no more than before. Another few days passed, and Juan stood on the patio looking totally different than the year before. His speech was not articulate, and no longer did he use any English. He was somewhat pale and seemed so much smaller. His gait was of a very old man. It was as though he had had a stroke, which I was soon to learn was true. He asked about a friend who had visited and then stumbled over to shake my hand. We spoke a bit, but something was missing. We said *adios* and then instead of walking to his house, he walked into mine and seemed to be looking for something. I realized he needed the *baños* and so I led him to it. He was in there for what seemed like an hour. His wife suddenly started calling for him. I went out and told her he was in my bathroom. She was horrified and said a few times she was sorry and would clean it. I tried to reassure her, but she was not happy. That's when I learned he had fallen ill and that's why things were not as they were before. I never saw Juan outside again.

After two weeks, another vehicle arrived; and suddenly, they were gone without even a good-bye this time. I made the assumption that the children came to take them back to the home in Jalisco. The house is very empty now, and I miss what was. I feel a loss in my life.

There is also Ana Maria. I met her chasing her dogs through the backyards. There are no fences and therefore no real privacy. People wander through all the time. Ana Maria stopped and introduced herself in somewhat broken English, but we were able to communicate fairly easily. In ten minutes, she invited me both to a benefit for poor children and to join her in her visit to her family the next day.

She is a middle-school teacher whose real passion is running around and saving stray dogs and cats. I heard lots of dogs barking ferociously in the middle of the night, starting a chorus of barking dogs. She had rented another house with a caretaker for all the dogs. The cats stayed in a kennel on the ranch of a friend in her family's village. There were at least fifty of the abandoned creatures under her care.

She was quite plain and somewhat tomboy-looking in appearance; and as far as my acquaintance with her went, she lacked a great sense of humor. She had never married and came from a very large family where somewhere way back, there were some political connections. She was always talking shop, mostly about the animals and how awful it was and the cost of her undertaking. Her family was apparently not happy about that and thought she was a bit mad. Her next-door neighbor, a man to be described next, only said negative things about her. She immediately went into showing me areas of the town to avoid because narcos lived there and it was dangerous. I was to get bars for the windows to avoid them from being opened and to keep my windows locked at night. I didn't abide by the last one. I'd die from the closed windows. Her car was always gone more than it was in her driveway so I assumed she spent a lot of time chasing the abandoned creatures.

The family was lovely and accepted me the day I visited, though most of the talk was family business and I didn't understand much anyway. I did get that two of the brothers were quite ill, one in terminal stage. There were lots of little children happily running around, and it was that close kind of family gathering I anticipated in Mexico—very casual.

After that, I socialized with her very little, nothing to do with not wanting to. It just didn't happen. She always seemed busy but always stopped to say hello and chat a few minutes when we passed each other. Each time I invited her to come over and have a drink, but she never did.

When I returned after my long absence, I didn't see her for two weeks. In fact, I wondered if she still lived here. One day, after a month, she drove through the gate as I was going in the other direction. We stopped and chatted for a few minutes. Her brother had died, and she had picked up a viral disease months ago and was still not well. She had to give up all the animal sheltering and looked very flat and sad. I invited her over to talk, but she has yet to come. Her car is mostly in her driveway except during her teaching hours.

And then there was Julio, her neighbor. I actually met him first, and he took any invitation to come and have a beer or two or three or ten. He passed by the first time when I was out in front of the house washing my car. He stopped to talk and never quite left, at least not for a few hours. He was fluent in his English, no communication problems there. He was fifteen years my junior and was quite the charmer. He was a developer and had a grand scheme he was more than willing to share. He was also willing to share on our first encounter that the recession and inability to get the necessary loan at the moment was making things a bit uncomfortable.

The conversation, with each cerveza, deteriorated a bit. I was lovely, I had fantastic legs, and I didn't look a day older than 40. Why didn't I have a man? He could satisfy me. He was divorced and rarely saw his only young daughter. Poor him! Not being one to want to hurt anyone's feelings, I let him ramble on, occasionally trying to change the topic back to him and his dreams of his development. When he got around to the sleeping with him, I sent him packing.

But he came back many a time. He actually was very interesting before the first six-pack was finished. He was the son of a general and had been "physically abused" by him. I put that in quotes because the definition thirty years ago and now is quite different. He may simply have had his mouth washed out with soap for saying "shit." I learned to send him home with excuses after the conversation came back to my sexual needs as perceived by Julio.

On one visit, he brought over the plans for his development scheme and offered me a small partnership to design and set up a medical clinic within the development. He said he would return with a contract, and that was the last time I saw him. And there was I looking forward to that contract! I believe he now no longer lives in the community. The house looks vacated without the car in his driveway. Maybe he's living in a trailer on the development site.

Guess I'm back to square one for meeting neighbors.

A Different Kind
of Pumpkin Patch

A special part of living in Puerto Vallarta, a resort city, is a trip into the countryside to explore and to mingle with the real people. The Sierra Madres surround the city to make a majestic backdrop. I often look toward the mountains and wonder what lies up there. There are small roads everywhere leading in the eastward direction to other towns and villages and waterfalls and gardens and accessible for a day trip. And finally, I did start exploring. My friends and I decided on a day trip to San Sebastian, a two-hour drive into the mountains almost directly east toward Guadalajara. My friends included a married couple from Canada and a Mexican, Arturo, who seems to know someone everywhere and always leads us to some special experience. He never fails to let us down, and he didn't this particular outing either.

The road to San Sebastian goes through a few small towns typical of the places just outside of the cities. There are the taco stands and small houses, several small *mercados*—the local small grocery stores. There are always a few *hombres* with sombreros riding on their horse or mule along the road. There's the occasional old pickup with a horse or mule or twenty people riding in the bed. Once past the outskirts of the city, the road becomes windier and rises in altitude. There are fewer vehicles and people on the road. The bush becomes denser and the air, cooler. The air smells fresh and clean, and the skies just seem bluer. The shops disappear, and there is the occasional stand where a local is selling fruits or vegetables direct from the farm.

The pumpkins were evidently in season because that was what was on display, and they were huge pumpkins, certainly would win a contest for size in our countries. I decided then and there I would buy a small one if one could be found to take back to make one of my favorite recipes, a pumpkin mushroom risotto, and no, it's not a Mexican dish. In fact, I wonder if they even cook anything with pumpkin because I've not seen that on any menu. And this was March, definitely not the Halloween season. Just before the final climb into San Sebastian, there was a blue farm-type house on the side of the road with a huge pile of pumpkins stacked in front. There was no sign saying, "*se venda*" (for sale), but we thought we would stop and ask on our way out of town.

On the route, a tequila distillery came into view. When in Mexico, do as the Mexicans and so we stopped for a bit of the tasting. Distilleries have popped up everywhere. I suppose it's like wineries in the Napa Valley or the south of France. Everyone here seems to be so eclectic so it was not only a distillery, but there were lovely rustic rooms to rent, not cheap by any standards, and a restaurant. The owner was more than welcoming and, of course, someone who knew Arturo's family. Annette, my Canadian friend, loved flowering plants and always delays us with her oohs and aahs. By the time we left, she had a few cuttings of their white geraniums and a few others plants. There wasn't a limit on the tequila tasting, but we had a whole day ahead of us so we limited ourselves.

We arrived in San Sebastian before noon, and I fell in love again. The "Lonely Planet Guide" has been my bible since traveling became my profession, but to date, I hadn't visited one of those picture-perfect little traditional Mexican towns with the colonial architecture, and here it was. The central square had the park in the middle with the white lace-like gazebo platform. There was a rose garden all the way around. The two-story connected buildings formed a square; every structure was painted white. The roofs of the buildings were all adobe-tiled. All the streets were cobblestone. The church was adjacent to the main square. Its steeple view seemed to blend into the surrounding mountains.

The entire town was pristine and well-maintained. There were many quaint little restaurants and historical hotels in perfect nick with traditional furniture and beautiful little garden patios. So many things grow there because of the exquisite climate. There were gnarled trees covered in orchids. Citrus trees abound, and the lemons looked as big as grapefruits. I tasted various fruits that looked like lemons, but all had different tastes.

We stopped to eat at one of the charming little restaurants. It was owned by an Italian and his Mexican wife. He made his own wine, which was extremely palatable, his *limoncella* (a beautiful Italian lemon liqueur), and of course, the fare was Italian and, I must say, the best Italian I've ever eaten. I've traveled throughout Italy on many occasions. Who'd have guessed that in Mexico?

San Sebastian is known to those who live in the Puerto Vallarta area, and it has been discovered by the expats. This leads me into the immigration issue that has plagued the U.S. government for so long. Now I look around here in Mexico. There is nowhere you can go, at least in the coastal areas where the Americans and Canadians have not come in droves. The village I live in probably is one-third expats, and it's far from the maddening crowd. San Sebastian is even further but had a fair representation. My question is: "Why don't we open the borders?" There's as many of us wanting to live down here as there are Mexicans wanting to go to the US. At the moment, San Sebastian is still a hidden secret and not inundated with tourist buses. I doubt that will last for long.

A few tequilas later, with Annette as our designated driver, it was time to return to the city. We stopped at the blue house pumpkin patch, and this is when the real day began. We were greeted by a middle-aged soft-spoken Mexican woman and her father who was almost hidden on the front porch by the plants, which were abundant. They were more than happy to sell us their pumpkins, though when I selected my small one, the old man laughed and said, "You can just take it." We started talking through Arturo and suddenly we were special guests and part of the family. Annette and I were looking at the garden and all the orchids and roses growing wild with awe. We could buy anything we wanted, the daughter said after consulting with her dad. Suddenly, the bottle of *recclia* (like tequila but made from another type of agave than the blue) appeared.

And the afternoon turned into magic. The mother who was deaf came out and was delighted to see guests. Both the old man and woman were a deep sun-tanned brown with very smooth skin. They were in their eighties, though one would never put them there. They didn't join us in the *recclia* because both were on medications, but they enjoyed watching us. We learned about the family, and they learned a bit about us. It was one of those moments when there were so many things I wanted to say and ask but couldn't because my *Español* was at the beginning stages.

In the end, we really did have to leave to return before dark with a promise to return and visit. We picked out some orchids for purchase, and they wanted no money for them. We left money anyway. Arturo told us they would be insulted but it was OK to leave it anyway because they could use it.

And so ended a very special day. We all agreed that it's those kind of moments that are so much more valuable than looking at a building or other historical sight. It is the people that matter.

WAR WITH THE ANTS

I bought my house in Mexico two years ago, Le Cruz de Huanacaxtle (a real mouthful) near lovely Puerto Vallarta. Little did I know that huge families of black army ants had been squatters for years. There were also the wee sugar ants, but they were fairly innocuous by comparison. I showed the army ants my papers proving ownership, but they simply ignored me and continued to march on, carrying bits of leaves from the honeysuckle and jasmine I'd planted on their backs. I tried discussing with them the concept of peaceful coexistence, but it went over their heads like water off a duck's back.

I finally went to the association management of the housing complex and discussed the issue with them. The manager simply looked at me with a smile and said, "Don't worry. They are only leetle ones." It took me back to my first trip in Mexico many moons ago when Cancun was only a thought for development and I sat down to dinner and on the table was a bowl half full of sugar and half full of little sugar ants. I called the waiter over, and he said the same thing to me then. Are we the only people in the world obsessed with not wanting to cohabit with the little creatures?

Being a hater of chemicals other than alcohol, I spoke with all the organic folks who were acquaintances. There were lots of ant-friendly suggestions. One was covering the base of the plants with coffee grounds. For some reason, this is a bit like gravel on the feet to us. Another suggestion was grits, which basically was the same kind of rationale, but grits are not a Mexican thing and a bit hard to find. Another suggestion was a combination of rubbing alcohol, dish soap, and water in a spray bottle. Supposedly, the ants don't particularly care for showers. I tried them all but my squatters were stubborn little bastards. I put away all the food, cleaned the dishes the second I finished with them, and wiped down everything. I'd turned into an obsessive-compulsive freak. But the ants marched on, carrying the fruits of my labor in the garden on their backs and occasionally looking up and sneering at me.

I went to sleep initially solving the problem of the ants. I stopped hearing the relaxing sounds of the tides rolling in and the mariachi music coming from the local restaurants nearby. An answer did not come in my fretful sleep. All I could envision was the marching ants carrying off my bushes and trees, a military battle song playing in the background. Eventually, the dreams became nightmares. I would see millions of the little devils lined up on my bed, glaring at me. Each night, they became larger, and their glares, fiercer. I had images of their homes under the ground, layer upon layer, and they continued to dig down more layers. It was like a massive beehive under my house, and I wondered how long it would take before the house would cave into the fragile ground. I woke up in the morning exhausted, and the bed looked like a war zone. I decided that it was necessary either to take more drastic measures or to sell the place and find another. I chose the first because I felt this is one time I should be in control. I needed to stop being the nice guy.

To Home Depot I marched, a woman with purpose straight to the garden department. I looked at the powder for *hormigas* (ants) and the spray stuff that kills anything that moves. There were a lot of choices. It was all written in Spanish of course so I just bought one of each, ready for the attack. The helmet, shield, and sword were ready. I donned my gear and paraded to the trail of ants. It was the spray first, less messy and less visible, and I didn't want anyone to know how cruel I had become. I then went and sat smugly in my lawn chair, reading my book, pleased that I no longer had unwanted visitors.

Each day, looking like Sherlock Holmes, I walked around the entire house, peering down into the multiple old ant holes, searching for new anthills and breathed a sigh of relief. I could once again go to sleep listening to the sounds of Mexico and then dream of more pleasant things. My focus of conversation was no longer the ants. I stopped boring my friends to death. The war was over, and I had triumphed, or so I believed.

One day, after a week had gone by, I was going on an outing to the botanical gardens to purchase more plants to replace the bare branches the ants had left me with. I went to the car, and lo and behold, there was a huge ant hill built up against my front tire and the trail of army ants was passing me, with bits of tender leaves and flower petals on their backs. They were daring me! The honeysuckle next to the driveway was bare. I ran inside like a madwoman, didn't bother with the gear, just got the can of very toxic white powder, and poured it down the holes and followed the trail, shaking the powder as I went.

The ants fell, one after another. It was a mass killing. After a few choice words, I went off in the car.

I checked again when I returned in the evening, and no ants. I got them this time. Another week went by and, yes, another anthill against the tire of the car. I had no new tricks up my sleeve. I was defeated. I went to the terminator and chose not to hire him when he explained all the weapons he had on hand to eliminate ants. There wasn't anything I hadn't tried yet. Week after week, the same thing happened, and week after week, the powder and sprays came out. It was a long drawn-out war without an end in sight.

My weekly grocery list included ant killer. I simply replaced plants when they no longer reproduced their leaves and my lawn was a mine field of ant mounds. I go through the same fury when I see a new mound, but I sleep at night. I realized defeat, and this is what came with the territory. I figure when the house caves into the hives below, the insurance will pay for a new house and the elimination of the ants. So we live in not so peaceful coexistence. I prefer the ants rather than the cockroaches the size of a saucer or the scorpions that bite.

Noise. Or Is It?

I've returned to Mexico, and the humidity is totally welcome. After all, it helps to maintain younger skin. The ants were there squatting on the property, their new homes underneath my car towered up to a foot high. I had to shovel before moving the car, and today I've returned to being a killer again, as expected. But there was something I totally forgot about and wasn't prepared for after all the quiet places I visited during the summer. The firecrackers were exploding at irregular intervals the moment I arrived. Knowing they weren't to welcome me, I asked about the event as I'm still not familiar with all of the festive occasions in Mexico. There are too many to count. I learned that it was a religious holiday, a tribute to the Lady of Guadalupe, and it would continue to the twelfth of December. It is now the twenty-sixth of October. It is obviously a jubilant time with the sound of parades followed by celebrations with drinking, dancing, and music into the night. Will I last the six weeks?

Noise, or at least what we "Westerners" define as noise, seems to be the common link, although varied, in all developing countries. Or could it possibly be that what is noise to one man's ear is music to another? The *Oxford Dictionary* defines *noise* as a sound, one that is especially loud and unpleasant. That indicates to me that it is still in the ears of the beholder. I love music and listen to most styles, but heavy metal and rap sound like noise to me. My neighbor would have a hissy because that's music to his ears, and so it goes with many sounds. I suppose one of the benefits of traveling is that we are exposed to the cultural differences in what is music to one's ear and what is alarming, bothersome, irritating, painful, and just plain offensive to another.

I arrived in Burundi several years ago for a medical mission, high in the remote mountains toward the Rwandan border. It was my first experience living in the more central part of Africa. I didn't sleep much in the beginning. Birds of every variety started chirping and tweeting and crowing at the break of dawn. Fine on a workday, saves needing an alarm; but on the weekend, I'm sorry, no! I have always loved the sound of the birds so never considered it noise. The local inhabitants certainly didn't either. It was a signal to start the fires and prepare for the day. But some of my compatriots couldn't have survived without their earplugs.

The security guards would turn on their satellite radios full blast shortly before dawn. The news and music would blare. And even worse than that, on Sundays, our only day to sleep in, all the churches would blare out gospel music from loudspeakers. I remember one Sunday morning, very, very early, we were sitting in silence in the common area, our entire team scowling. There wasn't anyone in our group who considered that music. The local people on the other hand are all very religious, and their style of practicing their religion was quite different than ours. The missionaries must have had least recognized that to covert, they needed to allow local cultural practices. Whatever the Christian denomination, the service is comprised of lots of singing and dancing around the church and so the gospel music is very much a part of that. It is communal. One sees the locals all dressed in their finery, little girls in organza dresses, boys in suits, strolling the dusty roads to their mud brick church with a thatched roof, primitive benches, and open spaces for windows and doors.

I reported on our incident involving a gunshot in another story about Burundi. The sound of an AK rifle in a house that you are in is deafening and yes, noise to anyone. A month after the incident when the dust had settled, I woke suddenly one night to what sounded like gunshots in the village. The feeling of terror engulfed me again, and I was out of bed, listening through the window and prepared to duck or run. There were no screams, and no one else in the house stirred. I began to wonder if I was hallucinating. I learned the following day that there had been a local wedding and the shots I perceived as gunshots had been fireworks. Noise to me but a celebration of joy to those attending the wedding. The thing is that noise or pleasurable sound is not only cultural but also related to previous conditioning.

My Congolese experience came only a year later so I was prepared for the roosters and the early morning village waking sounds. I had not been prepared for the drums beating, often throughout the nights, or the screaming and wailing after a death in the village, which went on until the body was in the ground. The drumbeat was often a message and the locals were aware by the rhythm of the beat what it meant. It might be the announcement of a death or it might be a joyous celebration or it might be something quite different. It was not noise but a means of communication. Normally, since I have traveled extensively, I'm able to tune out all the various sounds after a week or two, but in the Congo, it took six weeks before I slept soundly through the night. I guess it took longer because both symbolized a possible ominous message.

A few years earlier, I worked in Riyadh, Saudi Arabia for over two years. It is where the sounds are totally different. Saudi is a fundamentalist Muslim country, the place of Mecca and pilgrimage, somewhat a parallel of Rome to Christianity. No other religion is tolerated or allowed practice legally here. The call to prayer is five times a day, the first before daybreak. The chanting is done from the minaret tower above the mosque through a loudspeaker. I lived in a compound for the foreign workers, and we were surrounded by three mosques, none of which had synchronized clocks. When you work a ten-hour day, to be awakened two hours earlier than necessary was pure pain. To me, that was noise. My guess that to those who are not allowed to think differently, that was noise. The prayer calls were announced over the speaker system at the workplace as well. The Saudis would stop their work and attend prayers. The call went on for several minutes and was a disturbance to those of us concentrating on the job itself. But it is their religion and their ritual and who am I to label it noise when I am a visitor in another country? I have visited many other Muslim countries and have never found it to be so intrusive. Perhaps the noise perception is also linked to negative emotions about something or someone, in this case, the lack of the right to make choices.

There had been terrorist bombings of several Western compounds in Riyadh shortly before I arrived. In one in particular incident, several people were killed. Many families of foreign workers returned to their home countries. The atmosphere was still tense, and all the workplaces that employed Western workers had increased security. There were many nights in the beginning when I would lie in wait for the sound of explosives, and any popping sound would send me reeling to the floor, splayed out. What would have been normal sounds became exacerbated through fear. It faded away when nothing happened, and I acknowledged to myself the fear wasn't based on anything real.

And now, here I am back in Mexico. As this is where I live more than half the year, the sounds are becoming more familiar. My village does not have high buildings so sound travels. I can hear the mariachi music coming from the local bars and restaurants. The dogs still bark in chorus. I hear the parties and laughter from the surrounding homes, and I no longer consider this noise. It is more the sound of belonging and familiarity. Families stay up very late, especially on the weekend and so I've changed my schedule. I stay up late and sleep in late. There are still noises which seem to bother only me—the sound of the boys and their toys. I live in a gated community where maintenance of the grounds is provided. The staff has the lawn mowers, weed whackers, and vacuums. I don't know where they come from, but whoever designed them was into LOUD. And they seem to whack, cut, and suck it up at the most inopportune times. I still cringe, and closing all the windows doesn't help. That type of noise seems to carry out in the big macho trucks without mufflers. Maybe it's noise to the Mexicans as well, and they're simply more polite and accepting than we are, and that is cultural.

DONE WITH RICE AND BEANS

It was four months of rice and beans as an accompaniment to every meal, but I've returned from Central America never to eat rice and beans again. Living in Mexico gives one an appreciation of spicy food, but one must leave that appreciation at the border. The food gets blander the further south one travels. It was even difficult to find salsa. Granted each country had their own unique dish—and indeed some were tasty—but the beans and rice were the staple everywhere. I returned a few weeks ago, and I rekindled the interest in cooking myself.

I think the other thing I will avoid for a very long time is buses. We traveled anywhere from a couple of hours to a grueling eighteen-hour bus trips. All of the countries did have the first-class buses with seats, if they weren't broken, that went back to about a sixty-degree angle. "Broken" was the key word. Air-con was not optional and set at freezing. I bought a heavy wool serape in Oaxaca before leaving Mexico and probably would have died of pneumonia otherwise. The first-class buses always had toilets aboard but often ran out of paper and water a couple of hours into the journey. One bus company handled that by locking the door and the spare driver came back and unlocked it each time someone needed to use it. Some of the national buses did not have toilets and would move up to six hours without stopping. We often had the discussion on whether or not the locals had bigger bladders than us. We also used the chicken buses for shorter hauls. They are the old American school buses which have been painted up in brilliant colors but are otherwise falling apart. And at times, we ended up in the back of pickup trucks with mobs of locals when there was no other transportation.

And now, I say it was an amazing adventure, and I wouldn't trade a bit of it. People have asked what my favorite country is, and my response is that I loved each and every one for different reasons. Antigua and Lake Atitlan in Guatemala were beautiful, and there were so many handcrafted items made by the Mayan women and sold for next to nothing. The Pyramids at Tikal are a must. El Tunco (the pig) beach in El Salvador was lovely and not taken over by tourists. The Bay of Islands in the north of Honduras was extremely charming, and Copan in the hills is where I spent a week studying immersion Spanish. While there, a Mayan festival was held—the crowning of a Mayan princess. There was no alcohol at stands on the plaza, but everyone totally got into it. We were amazed by that. How do you have a party without alcohol? But they did and seemed to enjoy it as much as we do ours. There was dancing in the street. In Nicaragua, we looked down into a steaming volcano, spent almost a week in Granada, a wonderfully restored colonial city, and then spent a few days on Ometepe, an island with two volcanoes which are in the middle of Lake Nicaragua. Costa Rico was extremely expensive and Americanized but teeming with nature. We went to three of the national parks, and there was no counting the unique creatures we saw in nature just strolling along. Panama was the favorite for a short while. We arrived for Carnival and couldn't bring ourselves to leave until it was over. Old Town in Panama City reminded me of New Orleans. The Panamanians love to drink as much as the folks in New Orleans. The Panama Canal was amazing, and we saw it in a boat, on the Panama Railway, and from the Mira locks just outside Panama City. We finished with Panama visiting Boca del Torres, the island for a few days. It was of a different intensity and a lot more relaxing. Belize was less natural and a far poorer country than I had anticipated but still worth a visit. We went tubing through the caves, something Belize is known for. I felt it was way overrated. The pyramids at Lamanai (means "submerged crocodile") in the jungle were not overrated. It was the last pyramids that we visited, and we felt each site was totally unique to the others. We also visited a lot of cities in Mexico and flew to Havana, Cuba for a week. It was my favorite adventure particularly since it was illegal. I've always enjoyed rebelling—never too old for that.

We slept in so many different kinds of beds. It was not funny. We were in everything from new three-star hotels to whorehouses (didn't do any business though). We had probable bedbugs in one, and a rat chewed through my traveling mate's small backpack to get to some snacks in another. Some rooms were small but had huge verandas with amazing views. We stayed in one family-run place where the man would bring us coffee the minute we stepped out the door and would wait up until he knew we were safely tucked in our room. Until Mexico, hot water was always advertised but never was offered.

No matter what the room, we averaged about 12 to 15$ per day. There was just never any consistency to what that amount might buy in a room. Anyway, one of the fun parts was the anticipation of what we might find, though I preferred to avoid the rats and bedbugs.

We climbed volcanoes, rode horses, hiked a lot of miles or kilometers. My mate did the canopy thing. We went to a few ballets, heard a big variety of music but the wonderful music happened more in Mexico when we walked into Puebla unknowingly to a cultural festival and to San Miguel de Allende for *Semana Santa* (Holy Week) where the parades and sound and light shows on the cathedral was a nightly occurrence. We actually missed very little.

I must write a paragraph on people. Whatever country, people were charming, helpful, wanting to talk, interested, and interesting. In many countries, when I've tried to use the local language, the response was in English. In Central America, they listened patiently and responded in Spanish. What I enjoyed the most was speaking in Spanish while the Spanish person spoke in English. The only exception to the rule was the taxi drivers. They were generally assholes, feigned not understanding and took us to hotels that we did not wish to go to.

I will finish by saying that I'm not a hedonist, though the trip was definitely a pleasure from the day I left to the day I returned. There were benefits: my Español is much improved; I discovered the pan flute music, which is so relaxing and easy to listen to. I learned the other side of our involvement in the politics of Central America and believe what bullies we've been. We met a couple of ex-intelligence people in two different countries, both with the same stories to tell. We're just as corrupt as the rest and need not point fingers at other countries, and that's another story.

FINALLY, CUBA

I especially enjoy traveling to places that are or have been off-limits to Americans. I think for most human beings, there is an allure for doing things or seeing places that are prohibited. It's that element of—whether it's something we enjoy or not—seeing if we can get away with it. I vaguely remember as a young person traveling in the sixties that China and Albania were written in as forbidden on passports due to the U.S. paranoia about communism. They were the countries I was most desperate to visit back then. I did finally get to China when they first opened their doors to tourism. I never did get to Albania. A bit later, it was Vietnam, and I saw that too before the tourists arrived en masse. One country still on the list was Cuba. Old grudges die hard. I decided I needed to visit it while it was still Castro's Cuba; and gleefully, I broke the law.

Although the doors have been opened only for Cuban-Americans who have families remaining in Cuba and in special circumstances for study and other purposes with permission of our government, there is a continuous flow of Americans who visit by entering either through Mexico or Canada. The Cuban government is more than happy to have us spend our money and has been kind enough to avoid stamping the US passport. The figures I've read vary, but it's somewhere upward of eighty thousand Americans who go to Cuba without our government's permission annually. I ran into as many Americans there as anywhere else I've chosen to visit and maybe more since it's not that many miles away. I've read in one guide book that there is both a significant fine and jail time if one is caught. I had an American friend in the seventies who spent a summer working in the sugarcane fields in Cuba, and she said she was followed by the CIA for the two years after. Another person I met related a story that her young niece was caught in the past decade and spent a night in jail, a lot of money on a lawyer, and still ended up with a fine of $70,000.

That aside, as I said, there are a lot of Americans running around Cuba. I chose to join in that quest and spent a week in Havana. I would have stayed longer, but I ran out of money, and Cuba is actually a fairly large island to get around. I ran out of money not because I'm poor but because if one is from the U.S., cash is the only tender. Cash machines abound but you cannot use a bank card from the US. Credit cards from the US are not accepted, and Havana is very expensive for the foreign tourist. I learned there were two currencies. The local Cuban dollar was worth a tenth of the tourist Cuban dollar. It was necessary to change foreign currency for the tourist Cuban dollar. Plainly, I had no idea things would be that expensive and did not bring enough cash. We spent our last couple of days in Havana to find the locals' places to eat and to have a beer.

Havana was everything I had imagined and anticipated and more. The main street in the old town, Obispo, was lined with the grand old hotels with large bars open to the streets and Cuban bands playing, one after another. One can't help swaying to the rhythm. The shops are filled with Cuban crafts and those things for which Cuba is known—cigars and rum and more cigars and rum. There are of course the schemers who try to get you over to their house for a dinner of lobster for $10 or take you to the "original" Havana Club and convince you to buy them drinks all afternoon or sell you the best and cheapest cigars in town. I think they were probably quite genuine, but if caught, they can be in trouble.

When one thinks of Havana, one imagines all the old cars from the fifties, and they are still there in abundance. Many look shiny and new. There are Chevrolets, Fords, Nashes, even the occasional Edsels. It's like one huge antique car show. The story I heard was each person is allowed only one car in their life so they really take care. Some are taxis so you can go back in time and take a ride.

There's the old town, the new town, and the area in the middle. The old town has been beautifully restored. There are squares and churches and an incredible number of historical buildings. Being in the old town, you would never know you're in a poor country. The new town is as it's called and is the area where there are mansions, parks, and diplomatic houses. The area in the middle is the most fascinating to me, though you're safest walking down the middle of the road to avoid a brick or chunk of cement dropping from a crumbling building. In general, the homes and building are in varying states of degeneration or renovation, and mostly the former. The structure themselves are grand, and I'm sure one day will look as the old town.

We stayed in the area and became very familiar with the streets and the very congenial people living there. Everyone was quick to stop and give information and help you reach your destination. The second day after we arrived, we were walking through the area to go to the old town and an elderly woman came up to us and told us to follow her. She had a room for rent. So we did. She took us up to her second-story flat in a lovely Victorian building and showed us a beautiful room, with lavish décor and adjoining modern bathroom for $10. The hotels in Havana are priced as the hotels in the U.S. so it was a bargain. We stayed the remainder of our week there. Our only obligation to her was to sit and chat over a cup of coffee, in Spanish, before leaving to play tourist for the day.

She was a recent widow, and her son, a teacher, lived with her. She was licensed to rent rooms and was meticulous about the necessary paperwork which went daily to some government office. She spoke happily about her life in Cuba, and we surmised that her husband had a professional position in the public sector. She certainly seemed well-off for Cuban standards with her large flat-screen TV and the décor in the apartment. She had a balcony overlooking the street. Across was a very grand dilapidated building which had one of the most expensive restaurants in Havana on the top floor. A movie called *Chocolat* was filmed there, and the restaurant continued to rest on those laurels. I spent a few hours out there, watching extravagantly dressed people arrive in taxis.

The other very interesting person we met in the area between was Tommy of ballet fame and about whom a film was made. We were walking in the neighborhood, observing the architecture and ambience and saw an unusually brightly painted house with antique ceramics in the windows. It looked like a museum and so I crossed over to learn more. A charming elderly man came out and invited us in and told us it was his home. We were welcome to wander through it. One wall was covered with photos of his days as a professional ballet dancer. He had traveled the world dancing. I think he was sad and missed his days as a well-known dancer. I left feeling a bit sad for him.

In my younger years, I read every book Ernest Hemingway wrote. The first love of my life was also a big Hemingway fan. We wrote pages back and forth about each Hemingway book as we read them. I had totally forgotten that Hemingway had spent a great deal of time and wrote a book there, *The Old Man and the Sea*. The Cubans have not forgotten that Hemingway spent time there; he gets more plaudits than Castro. He hung out in two bars. One was the El Floridita, and it was where he drank his daiquiris. The other was La Bodegita, where he drank his mojitos. I will never have a mojito anywhere else. Best I've ever had. It was one of the highlights for me.

I never did see Fidel Castro, and it was hard work seeing any images of him. I expected large posters and paintings on walls and billboards and statues, but no. There were far more posters of Che. The only visible thing was his book. I left asking people we met at the airport, "Why?" and had lengthy discussions. One conclusion was that he was still alive and the posters and statues would come after his death. But Cuba is still Castro's Cuba, and I'm glad to have seen it before he's moved on and the hordes visit.

A Four-Wheel-Drive City
of Two Million

I was called to go to Haiti to assist in the relief effort just after the 2010 earthquake, but just having returned from another such project, I just wanted a break and refused. Almost a year later, I was once again called to go to Haiti, this time to help with the cholera. I was somewhere in the remotes of Central America and, selfishly, not willing to put an end to that experience, and once again refused. But a few months later, the call came again, and I couldn't refuse. I was asked to come to Haiti for only five weeks as a replacement for a nurse who had left. I said yes before the person had completed asking the question. I could cope with a month, no matter what the situation. I was on the plane to Port-au-Prince less than a week later.

I'd heard about the devastation and the slow progress, but the shock factor on hitting the ground was there nonetheless. I did not expect the likes of the slum areas of India, but the first sight that caught my senses were the immense garbage piles with pigs, goats, and dogs eating on one side and humans rummaging through the pile on the other side. The ride to the office took over an hour through twisting, broken crowded streets up to the high hills. The tent cities for the displaced were vast and everywhere from the center of the city to various locations up the hills. Huge piles of rubble remained, and many homes and buildings were still untouched with several floors collapsed, one on top of the other and suspended over the adjoining land. My head couldn't get around the thought of how many bodies were still buried in that rubble; and that rubble was still there a year and a half later.

That's not to say that it was like the day after the earthquake everywhere. The further up the hill it was to Pietonville—the trendy area for the expats to hang out and socialize—the more rebuilding was happening. A Haitian acquaintance told me that actually quite a lot had changed in that area. Once upon a time, it had been mainly residential. It had far less damage than in other areas and many who had lost businesses in the affected areas moved up the hill and opened restaurants and shops. The choice of restaurants and bars was never-ending. Inside, they are full of expats, and one could totally lose sight of where they actually were. There is a Giant supermarket. Note I didn't spell "giant" with a small G because it wasn't giant but certainly it was not bad for Haitian standards. One could get almost anything there for a price. I picked up a packet of four small mandarins, and it was $10. I hardly thought I'd buy those. The wonderful mangoes and pineapples in season from the women on the street selling from baskets made a lot more sense. Food did not appear in short supply. There were many huge gated houses in good repair and rented at exorbitant rates to organizations and NGOs. There were a few people out there making some big bucks. Unfortunately one of them wasn't me, and certainly it wasn't those people living in tent cities. And there were still tent cities even in Pietonville.

Port-au-Prince is a sprawling city of over two million, amazing for being a city on an island not much bigger than half the size of Florida. There were never-ending throngs of people on the street, walking and dodging traffic. It seemed every inch of the city was covered with people, vendors with shoes, plants, bags, or whatever sat along the side or sold their wares under umbrellas, tents, or broken buildings. The cars, NGO vehicles, painted colorful minibuses, big transport trucks all fought for space on the narrow winding roads. I had a hard time believing there were any rules of the road. Vehicles would simply go where they could move even if it was the wrong lane so the daily standoffs happened. Who would give in first? The motorbikes were right in there with the rest. It was chaos, and aggression was the name of the game. The result was that a twelve-kilometer journey would take an hour to an hour and a half with the exhaust fumes and the dust and the stench from the canals littered with garbage and excrement. If the earthquake didn't get you, there was a high possibility that a car accident could.

The Haitians speak French, not Spanish as do the people of the Dominican Republic, which occupies the other half of the space on the island. Apparently the slave masters ended up in the Dominican and the slaves in Haiti. The Haitians have over a four-hundred-year colorful history with multiple conflicts and interventions from other countries. It was originally the Spanish who dominated the then French pirates and African slaves. In a treaty sometime during the 1600s, the Spanish took the Western part of the island. The rest remained under French control. The slave independence came in the early 1800s, but violence and corruption remained. There were interventions by the Americans and British during the 1900s and most recently, natural disasters. On one index, Haiti is the poorest country in the Americas, and on another, one of the most corrupt.

The surprise for me when I arrived in Haiti was the running water and electricity in the organizational housing and, best of all, the wireless! I'm always prepared for—though dreading the cold bucket showers and hole-in-the-ground toilets—more the norm on an assignment. Granted almost daily the electricity failed and unfortunately the first time it happened, I was in the process of unpacking with the flashlight still in the abyss of the suitcase; but a few swear words later, the lights came on again. It didn't take long to realize the electric was more from a generator than the city; the noise was the giveaway. As for hot water, we had it, but there was no need. It was July when I went, and the heat and humidity were almost unbearable. A cold shower was as close as I came to what we call air-conditioning. Maybe by the time I do this kind of thing again, even the volunteer organizations will have air-conditioned houses and swimming pools. I've heard them say some already do.

Gangs were active in a fairly large central area, and several killings a week was not unheard of. Kidnapping, sexual violence, general violence with lots of trauma was and probably still is very much a part of the scene. Security is pretty tight for most of the organizations. Certain areas of the city are prohibited for staff. It was pretty much only in an organization vehicle one could go out at night. We were only allowed out in pairs, a bit frustrating when you're an independent, free spirit. There were places I only had to look. No one had to tell me to avoid them. There was the possibility of having some kid put his hand through the window of the car if you had it open and grab your camera or bag, and it happened occasionally. Protests were a common sight, and one sure didn't want to be near that. There were safe areas with very nice restaurants and discos; they were frequented by the locals. At a disco one evening, I was chatting with one of the locals. We had our arms around each other's waists, and I realized he had a pistol in his back pocket. I was told it was a status symbol. Not for me, it wasn't. I didn't realize that after one too many rum sours I'd given him my phone number and so I spent the next few nights making excuses when he telephoned asking me to join him.

As for the health status and the reason I was called there, cholera was still present, no surprise if you had seen the filthy water and the garbage in the streets as well as the generally overcrowded conditions. But it was coming under control in the capitol by the time I arrived. HIV/AIDs is prevalent. We dealt with a lot of trauma and some sexual violence, not surprisingly. What was surprising to me was not seeing amputees and malnourished people running around. The majority seemed to appear healthy physically and generally clean. Maybe I wasn't there long enough to see some things because I couldn't help myself being obsessed with the physically appalling environment. I never carried a book or my iPod for the one-hour journey each day to the workplace; I had a movie out there in front of me. A friend who had been here for a year with different organizations said she frequently saw people with missing limbs. It was expected after such a devastating earthquake.

I loved staring out the vehicle window and discovered new sights each day. My favorite was the broom brigade. Each morning and every few blocks, there would appear a small group of ten or twenty, all carrying the handmade brooms and wearing the same straw hat with folded-up veranda and fringe, white T-shirt, and trousers or skirt of choice. They would either just stand leaning on their broom or start sweeping, each in different rhythms. Some would sweep with vigor, and others just held onto their broom and swayed. Somebody is paying for a cleanup, but me thinks it'll take more than that. I never did figure out why I saw them only in Pietonville and never in the center where it's badly needed. I think each person had no more than one square foot to sweep.

Then there were the cars parked for what must have been a long time. They had four flat tires and a coat of caked on dirt an inch thick. We drove basically the same route each day, and each day, more of the car was missing. One day after several weeks, it was all gone. In the beginning, I thought they were cars that had not been moved since the earthquake, but they would never last that long sitting there with lots of useful parts and things that could be sold on a vehicle.

There were the neighborhoods—some seemed barely touched by the earthquake, others simply devastated. The mansions somehow appeared to have less damage probably because they were structurally more sound, and I'm sure those with money can do the repairs more quickly. Some of the houses were part-house and part-tent. People appeared to live in the houses whether they were badly cracked and leaning with a wall or two missing anyway. I was simply amazed that people learned to cope living that way. I was later to learn that many of these places accommodated renters and the owners of the buildings felt no obligation to reconstruct; the renters stayed on in anything that was livable.

The work group was a mixed one, including the ages, the countries of origin, and always the personalities. There were some young feisty ones from South America and Greece, some less feisty—a bit older and more subdued and some older and quite subdued. The mix also included a couple of Americans and Europeans, but generally, everyone got on and was quite likeable. Always when living in a group, there's the annoying behavior. For me, the worst was just the waiting. The cars were to leave at certain times, and it took an hour to gather the mob. Somehow, a few always managed to suddenly get lost in the maze of work and forget the others were ready to leave. I'm a bit anal with time and went a bit insane almost every day at five in the afternoon. There was our youngest team member. Most of the team put in their iPods for the forty-five-to-seventy-five-minute ride home. Our young friend did the same and sang aloud to her music all the way home every night after work. There were the few who could make a one-hour meeting last over three, and that was after the workday was over. For a change, though, everyone on the team was somewhat well-mannered and cleaned up after themselves; and best of all, the smokers used ashtrays instead of the floor. Everyone was congenial and had a sense of humor. With that one element—humor—one can survive the worst.

It was certainly a different setting living in the capital in a project rather than in the middle of nowhere. In previous projects, I always had money left at the end but not this time. There were places to go and things to see. Haiti had some magnificent beaches within a couple of hours of Port-au-Prince, and going there was a favorite pastime on the weekends. It cost a fair amount to enter, but there were nice swimming pools, a beautiful long stretch of beach with chairs and umbrellas included, and tasty cardboard hamburgers if you got hungry. The Haitians continued in their crafts, even after the devastation, and one of the most well-known is the metalworks. There's a village outside of Port-au-Prince, Croix-des-Bouquets, where almost every house in the village was filled with artistic metal delights. There were masks and mirrors and candleholders, some just hammered, others brightly painted. The other favorite to shop for was their colorful paintings. We never got bored on the weekends, and for most, the money was spent long before the end of the month when the next few gouts (the local currency) came.

But it always came back to the reality of Haiti. The roads were mostly four-wheel-drive, meaning, you bump along through ruts incredibly deep. In an hour's drive, one bears not only the traffic without rules that are followed, but also the driver's play the rap that has "fuck" in every sentence—full blast, and the smell of burning plastic within the burning garbage permeates the air. And everyone just takes it in stride. The more aggressive drivers just missed pedestrians, dogs, and anything else that crossed their path. I always sat in the back, making the assumption that there was a better chance of survival in case of an accident, and I did survive. I also saw fewer of the near misses. The Haitian transport vehicles called tap-taps were brightly painted, many with "Trust in God" or "Thank you, Jesus" on the front. I presumed that meant that one didn't have to take any responsibility, and I sure couldn't figure out what they were thanking him for—what with the entire natural and other disasters which befell them. I sure as hell wouldn't have been saying "Thank you." I'd be saying, "How about a break?"

There appeared to me a bit of "lack of emotion" that becomes visible at times. And how could there not? Is it not a defense mechanism against anger? When we closed our facility, which provided care to a large population, there was little visible in facial expressions and reactions. They heard the message and walked away. It's not how most of us would react when we suddenly found we were jobless. The other thing that is simply accepted, though not always gracefully, is the fact that the looting happens almost instantly, and no one raises an eyebrow. It simply seems very tragic. Generally, the population appears happy and involved in community as anywhere else, but we saw the occasional person on the street who didn't cope. One day in the middle of a crowded busy area, a totally naked young man strolled along, talking and shouting to no one in particular. And no one noticed him really. People simply carried on with whatever they were doing.

It is the same with the houses still left in the condition they were at the time of the earthquake. The locals didn't often discuss the state of their country. It seemed just an acceptance of their fate. Most seem willing to work when work was available, but there seemed ennui in terms of looking beyond today. I left after having completed the task I went to do and without feeling any great hope for Haiti's future, and that's sad.

THE END FOR THE MOMENT

About The Author

**K**enna **Bifani** was born in Milwaukee, Wisconsin. She graduated from University of San Francisco in nursing and LSU-New Orleans with a Masters. Her first love is travelling and working abroad. She has worked as a professional nurse on 5 continents in countless countries, first after hitchhiking Europe in the 60's, then moving with her husband, a geologist and their two children for his employment. Many years later after a divorce, she returned to travelling and working in unique settings round the world. Two years ago she made her home in Mexico and began to write the short stories from her travels.

Writing a book was always her desire. In 1987, while living in London, she published a cookbook, "American Home Cooking" which includes narrative to explain the cultural influence of food in the United States.

She continues to both practices nursing in remote places with aid organizations and to write and send stories to her friends and family as she travels.